ILLUSTRATED DICTIONARY OF
ARCHITECTURE

ILLUSTRATED DICTIONARY OF
ARCHITECTURE
Ernest Burden

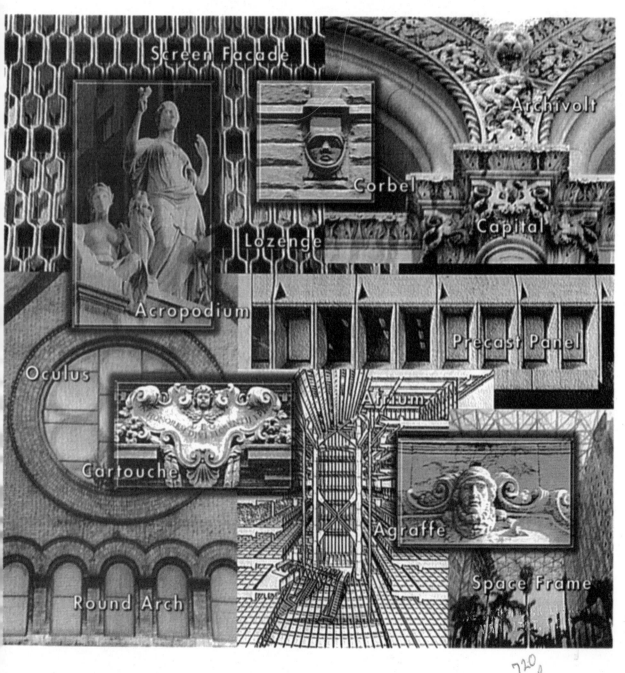

Library of Congress Cataloging-in-Publication Data

Burden, Ernest E.
    Illustrated dictionary of architecture / Ernest Burden.
        p.   cm.
    Includes index.
    ISBN 0-07-008988-4 (PBK)   ISBN 0-07-008987-6 (HC)———
    1. Architecture—Dictionaries. I. Title.
    NA31.B83   1998   98-4757
    720'.03—dc21   CIP

McGraw-Hill

A Division of The McGraw-Hill Companies

1 2 3 4 5 6 7 8 9 0 DOC/DOC 9 0 3 2 1 0 9 8

ISBN 0-07-008987-6 (HC)

ISBN 0-07-008988-4 (PBK)

Printed and bound by R. R. Donnelley & Sons Company.

PREFACE

Architecture throughout the ages has provided shelter from the elements, refuge and safety from intruders, palaces for royalty, shops for merchants, shrines for religious followers, and monuments for the dead. Throughout history all structures have been constructed with different designs, materials, forms, components and architectural styles. These items were all part of an integrated system of building representing the current customs of each culture.

The Egyptians had a relatively integrated system of building with simple parts, producing a sort of monolithic style, which featured highly carved ornamentation on the otherwise simple, massive forms. The Greeks developed a highly complex architecture, derived from wooden prototypes, that consisted of a "kit of parts" approach. It is this system that became the standard adopted by Western civilizations, and modified by succeeding generation into infinite variations of these basic forms. Other cultures, such as China and Japan, Thailand and India, developed similar stylistic features indigenous to their culture and religions. This dictionary describes all these styles, and illustrates many with photogaphs of typical structures.

The typical function of a dictionary is to isolate and define these elements, providing specialized information. This dictionary carries it to another level by illustrating definitions with photographs of elements in their position within structures. in addition, this dictionary shows several variations of the element, including historical and contemporary examples.

This dictionary has purposely avoided many archaic terms in favor of those that are in continued use throughout all cultures and times. The photographs also depict both historical and modern versions of the same component wherever possible.

The number of building components has not increased over the hundreds of years of building. In fact, the number has decreased as buildings become more simplified aesthetically. On the other hand, buildings have become more complex on the technical and functional level. These new technical terms have been included in this dictionary.

Architecture as such is a tangible product, and thus this dictionary illustrated with photographs adds a dimension previously missing in other reference materials using word definitions alone. However, there are also many intangible aspects involved in contemporary practice, and these have been listed as well. These include not only aspects of the design and building process, but many new terms relating to building renovation and restoration that are so prevalent in todays practice.

The 2,000 photographs in this book were selected from building sites around the world, some well known, others that simply provided the clearest illustration of the definition. No attempt was made to identify any of the subjects by building type, location, date, or architect.

Another distinctive feature of this dictionary is the clustering and cross-referencing of similar elements. There are over 40 grouped categories of definitions where one can find all related definitions, such as types of arches, doors, joints, moldings, roofs, walls, or windows. These grouped definitions are listed alphabetically under the main definition, and are also listed in the 2200 word index for easy location.

INTRODUCTION

The format is an easy reference guide consisting of two main categories of definitions: those that are illustrated and those that are not. The illustrated definitions are set into a single column of type adjacent to the first illustration, as per the following sample.

Abacus
The flat area at the top of a capital, dividing a column from its entablature. It consists of a square block, or one enriched with moldings. In some orders the sides are hollowed and the corners are truncated.

The definitions that are not illustrated are set into a wide column of type taking up one half the page, as per the following sample.

Acropolis
An elevated stronghold or group of buildings serving as a civic symbol; those of ancient Greek cities usually featured the temple of a deity, such as at Athens.

All historic styles are set into a wide column whether they are illustrated or not, due to the lengthy descriptions of those entries, as per the following sample.

Absolute architecture
A proposal made by Hans Hollien and Walter Pickler (1962) for a pure, nonobjective architecture. It was regarded as the antithesis of functionalism; its form would be dictated by the architect's individual taste and not by any utilitarian requirement.

The cross-referenced definitions included in the grouped categories have the word set in a smaller type size using all lower case letters. They follow the main listing in alphabetical order within that category, as in the following sample.

Arch
A basic architectural structure built over an opening, made up of wedge-shaped blocks, supported from the sides only.

acute arch
A sharply pointed two-centered arch whose centers of curvature are farther apart than the opening.

All cross-referenced definitions are listed alphabetically in the index at the back of the book.

A a

Abacus
The flat area at the top of a capital, dividing a column from its entablature. It consists of a square block, or one enriched with moldings. In some orders the sides are hollowed and the corners are truncated.

Abat-jour
A skylight in a roof that admits light from above; any beveled aperture.

Abat-vent
A louver placed in an exterior wall opening to admit light and air, but offering a barrier to the wind.

Absolute architecture
A proposal made by Hans Hollein and Walter Pickler (1962) for a pure, nonobjective architecture. It was regarded as the antithesis of functionalism; its form would be dictated by the architect's individual taste and not by any utilitarian requirement.

Abutment
A masonry mass, pier, or solid part of a wall that takes the lateral thrust of an arch.

Acanthus
A common plant of the Mediterranean, whose stylized leaves form the characteristic decoration of capitals of the Corinthian and Composite orders. In scroll form it appears on friezes and panels.

Accent lighting

Any directional lighting which emphasizes a particular object or draws attention to a particular area.

Accolade

A rich ornamental treatment made up of two ogee curves meeting in the middle, as found over a door, window or arch.

Accordion door See Door.

Acoustical door See Door.

Acoustical tile See Tile.

Acropodium

An elevated pedestal bearing a statue that is raised above the substructure.

Acropolis

An elevated stronghold or group of buildings serving as a civic symbol; those of ancient Greek cities usually featured the temple of a deity, such as at Athens.

Acroteria

A pedestal for statues and other ornaments placed on the apex and at the lower angles of a pediment; it often refers to the ornament itself that appears at these locations.

2

Acrylic fiber See **Plastic.**

Acute arch See **Arch.**

Adams style
An architectural style (1728–1792) based on the work of Robert Adam and his brothers, predominant in England and strongly influential in the United States and elsewhere. It is characterized by a clarity of form, use of color, subtle detailing, and unified schemes of interior design. Basically Neoclassical, it also adopted Neo-Gothic, Egyptian, and Etruscan motifs.

Addorsed
Animals or figures that are placed back to back and featured as decorative sculpture over doors, in pediments, medallions and other ornamental devices.

Adobe
Large, roughly molded, sundried clay units of varying sizes.

Adobe brick See **Brick.**

Aedicule
A canopied niche flanked by colonnettes intended as a shelter for a statue or a shrine; a door or window framed by columns or pilasters and crowned with a pediment.

Aegricranes See **animal forms.**

Aerial photo-mosaic
A composite of aerial photographs depicting a portion of the earth's surface; basic mapping information such as the name of towns and cities is usually added.

Affronted
Figures or animals that are placed facing each other, as decorative features over doors and in pediments.

Aggregate
Any of a variety of materials, such as sand and gravel, added to a cement mixture to make concrete.

Agora

An open public meeting place for assembly, often surrounded by public buildings, or marketplace in an ancient Greek city; the Roman forum is a similar example.

Agraffe

The keystone of an arch, especially when carved with a cartouche or human face.

Aisle

The circulatory space flanking and parallel to the nave in a church, usually separated from it by a row of columns; a walkway between seats in a theater, auditorium, or other place of public assembly.

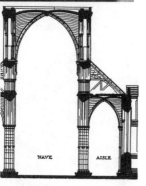

Alabaster   See Stone.

Alcove

A small recessed space, connected to or opening directly into a larger room.

Alignment

An arrangement or adjustment of forms or spaces according to a specific line.

Allegory

A figurative representation in which the meaning is conveyed symbolically.

Alto-relievo   See Relief.

Aluminum   See Metal.

Aluminum door   See Door.

4

Ambulatory corridor
A passageway around the apse of a church, or for walking around a shrine; the covered walk of an atrium in a cloister.

American School style
This style (1940–1959), characterized by the later work of Frank Lloyd Wright and the early work of Bruce Goff, represents the association of organic principles, such as the relationship of the part to the whole, self-sufficiency, rejection of tradition, free expression, and passion for the land.

Amorini
In Renaissance architecture and derivatives, a decorative sculpture or painting, representing chubby, usually naked infants; also called putti.

Amorphous
Those forms that do not have a definite or specific shape, or a distinctive crystalline, geometric, angular or curvilinear structure.

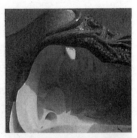

Amortizement
The sloping top of a buttress, or projecting pier, designed to shed water.

5

Amphitheater

A circular, semicircular, or elliptical auditorium in which a central arena is surrounded by rising tiers of seats; originally for the exhibition of combat or other events.

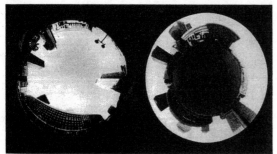

Analglyph   See Relief.

Anamorphous

A drawing which appears to be distorted unless it is viewed from a particular angle, or with a special device, such as an image viewed by a reflection in a curved mirror or anamorphic camera lens.

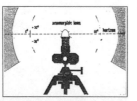

Anchor

A metal device fastened on the outside of a wall and tied to the end of a rod or metal strap connecting it with an opposite wall to prevent bulging; often of fanciful decorative design.

Ancone

A scrolled bracket or console in classical architecture which supports a cornice or entablature over a door or window.

Angle buttress   See Buttress.

Angle capital   See Capital.

Angle column   See Column.

Angle joint   See Joint.

Angle niche   See Niche.

Angle post   see Post.

Anglo Saxon architecture

The pre-Romanesque architecture (800-1066) of England before the Norman period is represented by this style, characterized by its massive walls and round arches and by timber prototypes translated into stone.

Angular

Areas formed by two lines diverging from a common point, two planes diverging from a common line, and the space between such lines or surfaces, whether on the exterior or interior of a structure.

Animal forms

The use of animals in natural or idealized form for ornamental details, such as sculptured or relief figures appearing on friezes, capitals of columns, and bas-relief panels.

aegricranes

Sculptured representations of the heads and skulls of goats and rams, once used as decoration on altars and friezes.

birds

Any member of the class *Aves*, which includes warm-blooded, feathered, vertibrates, with forelimbs modified to form wings.

bestiary

A collection of medieval allegorical fables about animals, each with an interpretation of its significance to good or evil; in medieval churches, a group of highly imaginative and symbolic carved creatures.

bovine

Any of the *bovine* mammal species, such as the ox and cow.

bucranium
A sculptural ornament representing the head or skull of an ox, often garlanded, frequently used on Roman Ionic friezes.

canine
Any member of the dog family, including wolves and foxes.

centaur
In classical mythology, a monster, half man and half horse; a human torso on the body of a horse.

chimera
A fantastic assemblage of animal forms so combined as to produce a single but unnatural design; a creation of the imagination.

eagle
Any of various large birds of prey, characterized by a powerful hooked bill, and long broad wings; used as emblems, insignias, seals, and ornamental sculpture.

feline
Belonging to the cat family; includes lions, tigers, and jaguars.

horse
A large hoofed mammal, having a short-haired coat, a long mane, and a long tail, and domesticated since ancient times for riding and to pull vehicles or carry loads.

VIRTUS

griffin
A mythological beast with a lion's body and an eagle's head and wings, used decoratively.

owl
Any of various nocturnal birds of prey, with hooked and feathered talons, large heads with short hooked beaks and eyes set in a frontal facial plane.

9

sphinx
An Egyptian figure having the body of a lion and a male human head; the Greek version featured a female monster represented with the body of a lion, winged, and the head and breasts of a woman.

Anta
A pier or pilaster formed by a thickening at the end of a wall, most often used on the side of a doorway or beyond the face of an end wall.

wivern
A two-legged dragon having wings and a barbed and knotted tail, used often in heraldry.

Antefix
A decorated upright slab used in classical architecture and derivatives to close or conceal the open end of a row of tiles covering the joints of roof tiles.

Annulet
A small molding, usually circular in plan and angular in section, encircling the lower part of a Doric capital above the necking; a shaft or cluster of shafts fitted at intervals with rings.

Antepagment
The stone or stucco decorative dressings enriching the jambs and head of a doorway or window; a door jamb.

Anthemion

A common Greek ornament based on the honeysuckle or palmette, used in a radiating cluster either singly on stele or antefix, or as a running ornament on friezes.

Antic

A grotesque sculpture consisting of animals, human and foliage forms incongrously run together and used to decorate molding terminations and other parts of medieval architecture.

Apex

The highest point, peak, or tip of any structure.

Apartment

A room or group of rooms, designed to be used as a dwelling; usually one of many similar groups in the same building.

Apartment house

A building containing a number of individual residential dwelling units.

11

Apex stone
The uppermost stone in a gable, pediment, vault, or dome, usually triangular, often highly decorated.

Applied trim
Supplementary and separate decorative strips of wood or moldings applied to the face or sides of a door or window frame.

Applique
An accessory decorative feature applied to a structure; in ornamental work, a design in one material cut out and affixed to another.

Apron
A flat piece of trim below the interior sill of a window, limited to the width of the window.

Apse
A semicircular or polygonal space, usually in a church, terminating an axis and intended to house an alter.

Arabesque
Generic term for an intricate and subtle ornate surface decoration based on a mixture of intermixed geometrical patterns and natural botanical forms used in Muhammadan countries.

Arbor
A light open latticework frame often used as a shady garden shelter or bower.

Arboretum
An informally arranged garden, usually on a large scale, when trees are grown for display, educational or scientific purposes.

Arcade

A line of arches along one or both sides, supported by pillars or columns, either freestanding or attached to a building. Applies to a line of arches fronting shops, and covered with a steel and glass skylight.

blind arcade

A decorative row of arches applied to a wall as a decorative element.

intersecting arcade

Arches resting on alternate supports in one row, meeting on one plane at the crossings.

Arcading

A series of arches, raised on columns, that are represented in relief as decoration of a solid wall.

Arcature

An ornamental miniature arcade.

Arch

A basic architectural structure built over an opening, made up of wedge-shaped blocks, supported from the sides only. The downward pressure is transformed into a lateral thrust, keeping the blocks in position, and transferring the vertical pressure of the superimposed load laterally to the adjoining abutments.

acute arch

A sharply pointed two-centered arch whose centers of curvature are farther apart than the opening.

13

barrel arch
An arch that is formed by a curved solid plate or slab, as contrasted with one formed with individual members or curved ribs.

basket handle arch
A flattened arch designed by joining a quarter circle to each end of a false ellipse; a three-centered arch with a crown whose radius is greater than the outer pair of curves.

bell arch
A round arch resting on two large corbels with curved faces.

blind arch
An arch within a wall that contains a recessed flat wall rather than framing an opening. Used to enrich an otherwise unrelieved expanse of masonry.

blunt arch
An arch rising only to a slight point, struck from two centers within the arch.

broken arch
A form of segmental arch in which the center of the arch is omitted and is replaced by a decorative feature, usually applied to a wall above the entablature over a door or window.

camber arch
A flat segmental arch with a slightly upward curve in the intrados and sometimes also in the extrados.

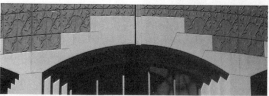

catenary arch
An arch which takes the form of an inverted catenary, i.e., the curve formed by a flexible cord hung between the two points of support.

cinquefoil arch
A five-lobed pattern divided by cusps; a cusped arch with five flioliations worked on the intrados; a cinquefoil tracery at the apex of a window.

circular arch
An arch whose intrados takes the form of a segment of a circle.

composite arch
An arch whose curves are struck from four centers, as in the English Perpendicular Gothic style.

compound arch
An arch formed by concentric arches set within one another.

corbel arch
A false arch constructed by corbeling courses from each side of an opening until they meet at a midpoint; a capstone is laid on top to complete it.

crescent arch
A type of horseshoe arch.

cusped arch
An arch which has cusps or foliations worked into the intrados.

depressed arch
A flat-headed opening with the angles rounded off to segments of circles; it was frequently used in the perpendicular style.

diminished arch
An arch having less rise or height than a semicircle.

15

discharging arch
An arch, usually segmental and often a blind arch, built above the lintel of a door or window to discharge the weight of the wall above the lintel to each side.

flat arch
An arch with a horizontal, or nearly horizontal intrados, with little or no convexity; an arch with a horizontal intrados with voussoirs radiating from a center below.

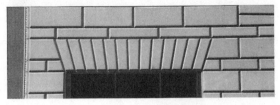

drop arch
A pointed arch which is struck from two centers that are nearer together than the width of the arch so that the radii are less than the span; a depressed arch.

elliptical arch
A circular arch in the form of a semi-ellipse.

equilateral arch
A pointed arch with two centers and radii equal to the span.

extradosed arch
An arch in which the extrados is clearly marked, as a curve exactly or roughly nearly parallel to the intrados; it has a well-marked archivolt.

false arch
A form having the appearance of an arch, though not of arch construction, such as a corbeled arch.

florentine arch
An arch whose entrados is not concentric with the intrados, and whose voussoirs are therefore longer at the crown than at the springing, common in Florence in the early Renaissance.

french arch
A flat arch with voussoirs inclined to the same angle on each side of a keystone.

gauged arch
An arch of wedge-shaped bricks which have been shaped so that the jambs radiate from a common center.

gothic arch
A pointed arch, especially one with two centers and equal radii.

groin arch
An arch formed by the intersection of two simple vaults; an arched extrusion of a cross vault.

16

haunch arch
An arch having a crown of different curvature than the haunches, which are thus strongly marked; usually a basket-handle or three-centered arch.

horseshoe arch
A rounded arch whose curve is wider than a semi-circle, so that the opening at the bottom is narrower than its greatest span.

inverted arch
An arch with its intrados below the springline, especially used to distribute concentrated loads in foundations.

lancet arch
Same as an Acute arch.

mayan arch
A corbeled arch of triangular shape common in the buildings of the Maya Indians of Yucatan.

moorish arch
The Islamic arch of North Africa and of the region of Spain under Islamic domination.

multicentered arch
An arch having a shape composed of a series of circular arcs with different radii, making an approximate ellipse.

obtuse-angle arch
A type of pointed arch, formed by arcs of circles which intersect at the apex; the center of the circles are nearer together than the width of the arch.

ogee arch
A pointed arch composed of reversed curves, the lower concave, the upper convex; a pointed arch, each haunch of which is a double curve with the concave side uppermost.

parabolic arch
An arch similar to a three-centered arch, but whose intrados is parabolic with a vertical axis.

pointed arch
Any arch with a point at its apex, characteristic of but not limited to Gothic architecture.

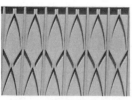

ribbed arch
An arch composed of individual curved members or ribs.

rigid arch
An arch which has no joints, and is continuous and rigidly fixed at the abutments.

Roman arch
A semicircular arch in which all units are wedge-shaped.

rampant arch
An arch in which the impost on one side is higher than that on the other.

round arch
An arch having a continuously curved intrados, often semicircular.

rear arch
An inner arch of an opening which is smaller in size than the exterior arch of the opening and which may be a different shape.

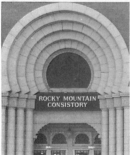

rowlock arch
An arch wherein the bricks or small voussoirs are arranged in separate concentric rings.

recessed arch
An arch with a shorter radius set within another of the same shape.

ROCKY MOUNTAIN CONSISTORY

relieving arch
A discharging arch.

rustic arch
An arch laid up with regular or irregular stones, the spaces between them filled with mortar.

segmental arch
A circular arch in which the intrados is less than a semicircle; an arch struck from one or more centers below the springing line.

semiarch
An arch in which only one half of its sweep is developed, as in a flying buttress.

semicircular arch
A round arch whose intrados is a full semicircle.

shouldered arch
A lintel carried on corbels at either end; a squareheaded trefoil arch.

splayed arch
An arch opening which has a larger radius in front than at the back.

squinch arch
A small arch across the corner of a square room which supports a superimposed mass above it.

stepped arch
An arch in which the outer ends of some or all of the voussoirs are cut square to fit into the horizontal courses of the wall at the sides of the arch.

stilted arch
An arch whose curve begins above the impost line; one resting on imposts treated as a downward continuation of the archivolt.

surbased arch
An arch having a rise of less than half the span.

three-centered arch
An arch struck from three centers; the two on the sides, have short radii; the center has a longer radius, and the resultant curve of the intrados approximates an ellipse.

three-hinged arch
An arch with hinges at the two supports and at the crown.

transverse arch
An arched construction built across a hall or the nave of a church, either as part of the vaulting or to support or stiffen the roof.

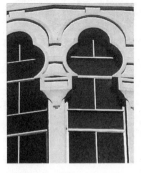

trefoil arch
An arch having a cusped intrados with three round or pointed foils.

triangular arch
A structure composed of two stones laid diagonally, mutually supporting each other to span an opening; a primitive form of arch consisting of two stones laid diagonally to support each other over an opening.

tudor arch
A four-centered pointed arch, common in the architecture of the Tudor style in England; a four-centered arch whose inner pair of curves is greater than that of the outer pair.

two-centered arch
An arch struck from two centers, resulting in a pointed arch.

two-hinged arch
An arch with two hinges at the supports at both ends.

venetian arch
A pointed arch in which the intrados and extrados are further apart at the peak than at the springing line.

Arched
Shapes formed by the curved, pointed, or rounded upper part of openings or supporting members.

Arched truss See **Truss**.

Architectonic
Related or conforming to technical architectural principles.

Architectural
Pertaining to architecture, its features, characteristics, or details; also to materials used to build or ornament a structure, such as mosaic, bronze, wood and the like.

Architecture
The art and science of designing and building structures, or large groups of structures, in keeping with aesthetic and functional criteria.

Architrave
The lowest of the three divisions of a classical entablature; the main beam spanning from column to column, resting directly on the capitals and supporting the frieze above.

Architrave cornice
An entablature in which the frieze is eliminated and the cornice rests directly on the architrave.

Archivolt
The ornamental molding running around the exterior curve of an arch, around the openings of windows, doors, or other openings.

20

Archway

A passageway through or under an arch, especially a long barrel vault.

Arcology

A conception of architecture (1969) involving a fusion of architecture and ecology, proposed by Paolo Soleri, an Italian architect in America. Arcology is Soleri's solution to urban problems. He proposes vast vertical megastructures capable of housing millions of inhabitants. One of Soleri's' visionary projects, Arcosanti, is now being constructed.

Arcuated

Based on, or characterized by, arches or archlike curves or vaults; as distinguished from trabeated (beamed) structures.

Areaway

A sunken area which permits access, air, and light to a lower basement door or window.

Arena

A space of any shape surrounded by seats rising in tiers surrounding the stage; a type of theater without a proscenium.

Armory

A building used for military training or for the storage of military equipment.

Arris

An external angular intersection between two sharp planar or curved faces, as in moldings or between two flutes in a Doric column.

Art Deco style

Stimulated by an exhibition in Paris, this style (1925–1940) drew its inspiration from Art Nouveau, Native American art, Cubism, the Bauhaus, and Russian ballet. The stylistic elements were eclectic, including austere forms. It was characterized by linear, hard-edge, or angular composition with stylized decoration. It was the style of cinemas, ocean liners, and hotel interiors. It was called "modernistic," and reconciled mass production with sophisticated design. Facades were arranged in a series of setbacks emphasizing the geometric form. Strips of windows with decorative spandrels add to the composition. Hard-edge, low-relief ornamentation was common around door and window openings and along roof edges or parapets. Ornamental detailing is either executed in the same material as the building, in contrasting metals, or in glazed bricks or mosaic tiles. The style was used for skyscraper designs like the Chrysler building in New York City.

Articulation

Shapes and surfaces having joints or segments which subdivide the area or elements; the joints or members add scale and rhythm to an otherwise plain surface.

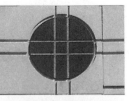

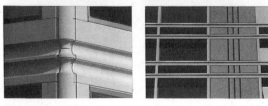

Artificial stone

A mixture of stone chips or fragments, usually embedded in a matrix of mortar, cement, or plaster; the surfaces may be ground, polished, molded, or otherwise treated to simulate natural stone.

Art Moderne style

A modern style (1930–1945), characterized by soft rounded corners, flat roofs, and smooth wall finishes devoid of surface ornamentation. A distinctive streamlined look was created by wrapping curved window glass around corners. Ornamentation consisted of mirrored panels and cement panels with low relief. Aluminum and stainless steel were used for door and window trim, railings and balusters. Metal or wooden doors often had circular windows.

Art Nouveau architecture

A movement (1880–1910) in European architecture and applied arts, developed principally in France and Belgium, characterized by flowing and sinuous organic and dynamic forms, naturalistic ornament and a strict avoidance of historical traits. Other names for the style include, Le Modern Style (France); Jugendstil (Germany), named after the German term for youth style; Stile Liberty (Italy), named after the Liberty and Company store in London; Modernismo (Spain); and Sezession (Austria), named after its proponents seceded from the Academy of Art in Vienna. The style drew on Baroque, Gothic and Moorish traditions, but was mainly unbounded by rules. Art Nouveau exploited the machine and reveled in the possibilities of decorative tiles and wrought iron. This was a deliberate attempt to put an end to imitations of past styles. In its place was a free type of architecture which integrated arts and crafts with architectural forms.

Arts and Crafts movement
A movement (1880–1891) which restored creativity to the decorative arts and indirectly to architecture. Architects such as Henry Van de Velde, Joseph Hoffman, and Charles Rennie Mackintosh had a very strong influence on this movement. It abandoned the stylistic imitation of the nineteenth century and laid the groundwork for the creative works of the Art Nouveau styles that followed.

Asbestos
A noncombustible, flexible fiber that is able to withstand high temperatures; it is fabricated into many forms, either alone or mixed with other ingredients.

Asbestos-cement board
A dense, rigid board containing a high percentage of asbestos fiber bonded with portland cement, noncombustible, used in sheet or corrugated sheathing.

Ashlar masonry   See Masonry.

Aspect
The point from which one looks, a point of view; a position facing a given direction, an exposure.

Aspect ratio
In any rectangular configuration, the ratio between the longer dimension and the shorter dimension.

Asphalt
A mixture of bitumens obtained from native deposits or as a petroleum by-product used for paving, water proofing and roofing applications.

Asphalt roofing
A roofing material manufactured by saturating a dry felt sheet with asphalt, and then coating the saturated felt with a harder asphalt coating, usually in roll form.

Asphalt shingles
Shingles manufactured from saturated roofing felt that is coated with asphalt, with mineral granules on the side exposed to the weather.

Asphalt tile
A resilient floor tile that is composed of asbestos fibers with asphaltic binders; set in mastic and installed over wood or concrete floors.

Assyrian architecture
Large palaces and temple complexes with ziggurats characterize this style (900–700 B.C.); the external walls were ornamented in carved relief or polychrome bricks. Doorways had semicircular arches with glazed brick around the circumference; windows were square-headed and high up in the wall. Interior courts were filled with slender columns with high molded bases, fluted shafts and capitals of recurring vertical scrolls. The bracket form of the topmost part was fashioned with the heads of twin bulls. They were widely spaced to support timber and clay roofs.

Astragal

A member or combination of members, fixed to one of a pair of doors or casement windows to cover the joint between the meeting stiles and to close the gap in order to prevent drafts, passage of light, air or noise.

Asymmetry

Not symmetrical, with the parts not arranged correspondingly identical on both sides of a central axis.

Atrium

The forecourt of an early Christian basilica, with colonnades on all four sides, and a fountain in the center. derived from the entrance court of a Roman dwelling, roofed to leave an opening to admit light. Rain was received in a cistern below. The modern version is a common public space with skylights in an office or hotel complex.

Atelier

A place where artwork or handicrafts are produced by skilled workers; a studio where the fine arts including architecture, are taught.

Atlas

A figure of a man used in place of a column to support an entablature; also called Atlantes and Telemon.

Attic

A low wall or story above the cornice of a classical facade; originally, a small top story representing the structure's termination against the sky, expressing the summation of the facade's design elements below.

Auditorium

That part of a theater, school or public building which is set aside for the listening and viewing audience.

Awning
A rooflike cover of canvas or other lightweight material, extending in front of a doorway or window, or over a deck, providi~~n~~ tection from ~~th~~

Awning window   See **Window**.

Axis
An imaginary straight line about which parts of a building or a group of buildings can be arranged or measured.

Axonometric perspective
A form of orthographic projection in which a rectangular object, projected on a plane, shows three faces.

Axonometric projection   see **Projection drawing**

Aztec architecture
An architecture (1100–1520) that emerged from the austere forms of the Toltecs, characterized by strong grid plans, monumental scale, and brightly colored exteriors, often with highly stylized surface carvings of human figures, floral patterns and gods. Pyramids often supported two temples with parallel stairways. Destruction by the Spanish left few remains, as the Aztec capital of Tenochtitlan is entirely buried under modern Mexico City.

B b

Babylonian architecture
An architecture (2000–1600 B.C.) characterized by mud-brick walls articulated by pilasters and faced with glazed brick. The city of Babylon contained the famous Tower of Babel and the Ishtar Gate, decorated with enameled brick friezes of bulls and lions, and the Hanging Gardens of Semiramis. The ruins of the Assyrian Palace of Khorsabad show evidence of monumental sculptural decoration. The Palace of Darius at Persepolis featured magnificent relief carvings.

Backband molding   See **Molding**.

Backing brick   See **Brick**.

Baffle

An opaque or translucent plate used to shield a light source from direct view at certain angles; a flat deflector designed to reduce sound transmission.

Balance

A harmonizing or satisfying arrangement, or proportion of parts or elements, as in a design or composition; the state of equipoise between different architectural elements.

formal balance

Almost always characterized by symmetrical elements.

informal balance

Designs where the forms are mostly asymmetrical.

Balconet

A pseudo-balcony; a low ornamental railing to a window, projecting but slightly beyond the plane of the window, threshold or sill, having the appearance of a balcony when the window is fully open.

Balcony

A projecting platform usually on the exterior of a building, sometimes supported from below by brackets or corbels or cantilevered by projecting members of wood, metal or masonry.

Ballflower

A spherical ornament composed of three conventionalized petals enclosing a ball, usually in a hollow molding; popular in the English Decorated style.

Balloon framing

A system of framing a wooden building wherein all vertical studs in the exterior bearing walls and partitions extend the full height of the frame from sill to roof plate; the floor joists are supported by sills.

Baluster

One of a number of short vertical members used to support a stair railing.

Baluster column

A short, thick-set column in a subordinate position, as in the windows of early Italian Renaissance facades.

Balustrade

An entire railing system, as along the edge of a balcony, including a top rail, bottom rail and balusters.

Band

A flat horizontal fascia, or a continuous member or series of moldings projecting slightly from the wall plane, encircling a building or along a wall, that makes a division in the wall.

Band

Banded rustication

Alternating smooth ashlar and roughly textured stone.

Banding

Horizontal subdivisions of a column or wall using a change in profile or change in materials.

27

Banderole ornament See Ornament

Band molding See Molding.

Bar molding See Molding.

Bar tracery See Tracery.

Bargeboard
A trim board used on the edge of gables where the roof extends over the wall; it either covers the rafter or occupies the place of a rafter; originally ornately carved.

Bargecourse
The coping of a wall, formed by a course of bricks set on edge.

Bargestone
One of the projecting units of masonry, which forms the sloping top of a gable wall.

Barn
A building for housing animals and storing farm equipment, hay, and other agricultural produce.

Baroque architecture
A style (1600–1760) named for the French word meaning bizarre, fantastic or irregular. It was the most lavish of all styles, both in its use of materials and the effects that it achieved. Mannerist styles were often adopted and carried to the extreme as bold, opulent and intentionally distorted . Pediments are broken and facades undulated, while interiors were theatrical, exhibiting a dramatic combination of architecture, sculpture, painting and the decorative arts.

Barracks
Temporary or permanent housing erected for soldiers or groups of workers.

Barrel arch See **Arch.**

Barrel roof See **Roof.**

Barrel vault
A masonry vault of plain semicircular cross section, supported by parallel walls or arcades, and adapted to longitudinal areas.

Bas-relief See **Relief.**

Bascule
A structure that rotates about an axis, as a seesaw, with a counterbalance equal to the weight of the structure at one end, used for movable bridges.

Base
The lowest part of a pillar, wall or building; commonly of the same form as the other moldings. In some styles the bases are more complex as they modulate between the floor and wall or column group above.

Baseboard
A flat projection from an interior wall or partition at the floor, covering the joint between the floor and wall and protecting the wall; it may be plain or molded.

Base block
A block of any material, generally with little or no ornament, forming the lowest member of a base at the foot of a door or window.

Base molding See **Molding.**

Basement
Usually the lowest story of a building, either partly or entirely below grade.

Baseplate
A steel plate for transmitting and distributing a column load to the supporting foundation material.

Basic services
The services performed by an architect during the following five phases of a project; schematic design; design development; construction documentation; bidding or negotiation; and contract administration.

Basilica
A Roman hall of justice with a high central space lit by a clerestory with a timbered gable roof. It became the form of the early Christian church, with a semicircular apse at the end preceded by a vestibule and atrium.

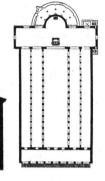

Basket capital See **Capital.**

Basket handle arch See **Arch.**

Basketweave bond See **Bond.**

Bath
An open tub used as a fixture for bathing; the room containing the bathtub; the Roman public bathing structure consisting of hot, warm and cool pools, sweat rooms, athletics and other facilities.

Bathhouse
A building equipped with bathing facilities; a small structure containing rooms or lockers for bathers, as at the seaside.

Batten
A narrow strip of wood that is applied over a joint between parallel boards in the same plane. In roofing, a strip applied over boards or structural members as a base for attaching slate, wood, or clay shingles.

Batter
A wall that gently slopes inward towards the top.

Battered

Those forms that slope from a true vertical plane from bottom to top, as in the outside surface of a wall.

Battlement

A parapet having a regular alternation of solid parts and openings, originally for defense, but later used as a decorative motif.

Bauhaus style

An architectural style developed at the school of design established by Walter Gropius in 1919 in Weimar, Germany; it moved to Dessau in 1926 and closed in 1933. The term became virtually synonymous with modern teaching methods in architecture and the applied arts and with functional aesthetics for the industrial age. It epitomized the marriage of modern design, mass production and industrial design.

Bay

A principal compartment or division in the architectural arrangement of a building, marked either by buttresses or pilasters in the wall, by the disposition of the main arches and pillars, or by any repeated spatial units.

The Atrium on Bay

Bay leaf garland See Garland.

Bay window See Window.

Bead molding See Molding.

Beak molding See Molding.

Beam

A rigid structural member whose prime function is to carry and transfer transverse loads across a span to the supports; as a joist, girder, rafter, or purlin.

box beam

One or more vertical plywood webs laminated to seasoned wood flanges. Vertical spacers separate the flanges at intervals along the length of the beam to distribute the loads and to provide stiffness.

camber beam

A beam curved slightly upward toward the center.

collar beam

A horizontal member which ties together two opposite common rafters, usually at a point about halfway up the rafters below the ridge.

crossbeam

A beam which runs transversly through the center line of a structure; any transverse beam in a structure such as a joist.

hammer beam

One of a pair of short horizontal members, attached to the foot of a principal rafter, located within a roof structure in place of a tie beam.

tie beam

In roof framing, a horizontal timber connecting two opposite rafters at their lower ends to prevent them from spreading.

Bearing wall See Wall.

Beastiary See animal forms

Beaux-Arts Classicism
Grandiose compositions with exuberant detail and a variety of stone finishes characterize this style (1890–1920). Classical colossal columns were grouped in pairs on projecting facades with enriched molding and freestanding statuary; pronounced cornices and enriched entablatures are topped with a tall parapet, balustrade, or attic story. It fostered an era of academic revivals, principally public buildings featuring monumental flights of steps.

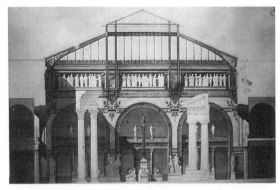

Beaux-Arts style
Historical and eclectic design on a monumental scale, as taught at the Ecole des Beaux-Arts in Paris, typified this style (1860–1883). It was one of the most influential schools in the nineteenth century, and its teaching system was based on lectures combined with practical work in studios and architectural offices. Its conception of architecture lies in the composition of well-proportioned elements in a symmetrical and often monumental scheme.

Bed mortar joint See Joint.

Belfry
A room at or near the top of a tower which contains bells and their supporting timbers.

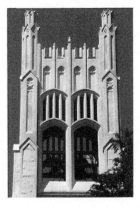

Bell
The body of a Corinthian capital or a Composite capital, without the foliage.

Bell arch See Arch.

Bell cage
Timber framework which supports the bells in a belfry or steeple.

Bell chamber
A room containing one or more large bells hung on their bell cage.

Bell gable
A small turret placed on the ridge of a church roof to hold one or more bells.

Bell roof See Roof.

Bell-shaped dome See Dome.

Bell tower
A tall structure either independent or part of a building used to contain one or more bells; also called a campanile.

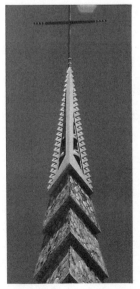

Bell turret
A small tower, usually topped with a spire or pinnacle, containing one or more bells.

Beltcourse
A projecting horizontal course of masonry, of the same or dissimilar material used to throw off water from the wall; usually coincides with the edge of an interior floor.

Belvedere
A building, architectural feature, or rooftop pavilion from which a vista can be enjoyed.

Bent
A framework, which is transverse to the length of a framed structure; usually designed to carry both a lateral and a vertical load.

Berm
The horizontal surface between a moat and the exterior slope of a fortified rampart; a continuous bank of earth piled against one or more exterior walls of a building as a protection against the elements.

Beton brut
Concrete textured by leaving the impression of the form in which it was molded, as when wood is used to create a grained surface effect.

Bevel
A sloped or canted surface resembling a splay or other chamfer, where the sides are sloped for the purpose of enlarging or reducing them.

Bezant
An ornament shaped like a coin or disk, sometimes used in a series in decorative molding designs.

Bi-fold door See Door.

Bi-lateral symmetry See Symmetry.

Bifron capital See Capital.

Billet molding See Molding.

Biotecture
A term (1966–1970) combining "biology" and "architecture," coined by Rudolph Doernach. It denotes architecture as an artificial "super system," live, dynamic, and mobile.

Birch See Wood.

Birds See animal forms.

Blank door See Door.

Blank window See Window.

Blemish
A minor defect in appearance that does not affect the durability or strength of wood, marble, or other material.

Blending
A gradual merging of one element into another.

Blind
A device to obstruct vision or keep out light, usually consisting of a shade, a screen, or an assemblage of panels or slats.

Blind arch See Arch.

Blind door See Door.

Blind joint See Joint.

Blind pocket
A pocket in the ceiling at a window head to accommodate a venetian blind when raised.

Blind story
A floor level without exterior windows.

Blind tracery See Tracery.

Blind window See Window.

Block
A masonry unit, or a solid piece of wood or other material; a large piece of stone, taken from the quarry to the mill for sawing and further working.

Block modillion See Modillion.

Blocking
Pieces of wood used to secure, join, or reinforce framing members, or to fill spaces between them.

Blueprint
A reproduction of a drawing by a contact printing process on light-sensitive paper, producing a negative image of white lines on a blue background; refers to architectural working drawings for construction.

Bluestone   See Stone.

Blunt arch   See Arch.

Board and batten
A form of sheathing for wood frame buildings consisting of wide boards, usually placed vertically, whose joints are covered by narrow strips of wood over joints or cracks.

Boat house
A structure for storing boats when not in use; generally built at the water's edge, often built partly over water; sometimes has provisions for social activities.

Bodhika
In Indian architecture, the capital of a column.

Bolection molding   See Molding.

Bollard
A low single post, or one of a series, usually of stone or concrete, set upright in the pavement, closely spaced to prevent motor vehicles from entering an area.

Bond
An arrangement of masonry units to provide strength, stability and in some cases beauty by setting a pattern of lapping units over one another to increase the strength and enhance the appearance, or by connecting them with metal ties; some units may extend into adjacent courses, or through the wall; the vertical joints are not continuous. The adhesion between mortar and the masonry units or with the steel reinforcement.

basketweave bond
A checkerboard pattern of bricks, laid either horizontally and vertically, or on the diagonal.

bull header bond
A brick header unit which is laid on edge so that the end of the masonry unit is exposed vertically.

bull stretcher bond
Any stretcher which is laid on edge exposing its broad face horizontally.

common bond
A bond in which every fifth or sixth course consists of headers, the other courses by stretchers.

diagonal bond
A type of raking bond in masonry walls, consisting of a header course with the bricks laid at a diagonal in the face of the wall.

dogtooth course
A stringcourse of bricks laid diagonally so that one corner projects beyond the face of the wall.

dutch bond
Same as English cross bond or Flemish bond.

english bond
Brickwork that has alternate courses of headers and stretchers, forming a strong bond which is easy to lay.

flemish bond
In brickwork, a bond in which each course consists of headers and stretchers laid alternately, each header is centered with respect to the stretcher above and the stretcher below it.

33

flemish diagonal bond
A bond in which a course of alternate headers and stretchers is followed by a course of stretchers, resulting in a diagonal pattern.

raking bond
A method of bricklaying in which the bricks are laid at an angle in the face of the wall; either diagonal bond or herringbone bond.

rowlock
A brick laid on its edge so that its end is exposed; used on a sloping window sill, or to cap a low brick wall.

running bond
Same as stretcher bond.

sailor
A brick laid vertically with the broad face exposed.

shiner
A brick laid horizontally on the longer edge with the broad face exposed.

skintled bond
Brickwork laid so as to form a wall with an irregular face, produced by the rough appearance of the skintled joints.

soldier
A brick laid vertically with the longer, narrow face exposed.

stack bond
In brickwork, a patterned bond where the facing brick is laid with all vertical joints aligned; in stone veneer masonry, a pattern in which single units are set with continuous vertical and horizontal joints.

Boom
A cantilevered or projecting structural member, such as a beam or spar, which is used to support, hoist, or move a load.

Border
A margin, rim, or edge around or along an element; a design or a decorative strip on the edge of an element.

Boss
A projecting, usually richly carved ornament placed at the intersection of ribs, groins, beams, or at the termination of a molding.

Bossage
In masonry, projecting, rough-finished stone left during construction for carving later in final decorative form.

Bovine See animal forms.

Bower
A rustic dwelling, generally of small scale and picturesque nature; a sheltered recess in a garden, a gazebo.

Bowstring truss See Truss.

Bow window See Window.

Box beam See Beam.

Box column See Column.

Box girder
A hollow beam with either a square, rectangular or circular cross section; sometimes vertical instead of horizontal, and attached firmly to the ground like a cantilever.

Box-head window See Window.

Box stair See Stair.

Brace
A metal or wood member used to stiffen or support a structure; a strut that supports or fixes another member in position or a tie used for the same purpose.

Bracing
See also: Cross bracing, Diagonal bracing, Knee bracing, Lateral bracing.

cross bracing
A pair of diagonal braces crossing each other to stabilize a structural frame against lateral forces.

diagonal bracing
A system of inclined members for bracing the angles between the members of a structural frame against horizontal forces, such as wind.

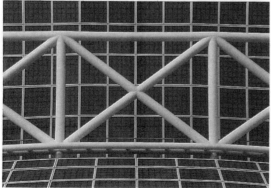

knee brace
A diagonal corner member for bracing the angle between two joined members; being joined to each other partway along its path serves to stiffen and strengthen the joint.

lateral bracing
Stabilizing a wall beam or structural system against lateral forces by means of diagonal or cross bracing, either horizontally by roof or floor construction or vertically by pilasters, columns or cross walls.

Braced frame
The frame of a building in which resistance to lateral forces is provided by diagonal bracing, knee-bracing or cross-bracing; sometimes using girts that are mortised into solid posts which are full frame height.

Bracket
A projection from a vertical surface providing structural or visual support under cornices, balconies, windows, or any other overhanging member.

Bracket capital See **Capital**.

Branch tracery See **Tracery**.

Brass See **Metal**.

Brattice
In medieval fortifications, a tower or bay of timber construction, erected at the top of a wall during a siege.

Breast
That portion of a wall between the floor and a window above; a defensive wall built about breast high.

Breezeway
A covered passageway, open to the outdoors connecting either two parts of a building or two buildings.

Brick
A solid or hollow masonry unit of clay mixed with sand, and molded into a small rectangular shape while in a plastic state, then baked in a kiln, or dried in the sun.

adobe brick
Large, roughly molded, sundried clay brick of varying sizes and thicknesses.

backing brick
A relatively low-quality brick used behind the face brick or behind other masonry.

clinker brick
A very hard-burnt brick whose shape is distorted, owing to nearly complete vitrification; used mainly for paving, or as ornamental accents.

common brick
Brick for building purposes not treated for texture or color.

face brick
Brick made or selected to give an attractive appearance when used without rendering of plaster or other surface treatment of the wall; made of selected clays, or treated to produce the desired color.

firebrick
Brick made of a ceramic material which will resist high temperatures; used to line furnaces, fireplaces and chimneys.

gauged brick
Brick which has been cast, ground, or otherwise manufactured to exact and accurate dimensions.

glazed brick
Brick or tile having a ceramic glaze finish.

king closure brick
A rectangular brick, one end of which has been cut off diagonally to half the width of the brick, it is used as a closer in brickwork.

modular brick
A brick with nominal dimensions based on a 4" module.

molded brick
Any specially shaped brick, usually for decorative work.

rustic brick
A fire-clay brick having a rough-textured surface; used for facing work; often multicolored.

Bridge
A structure which spans a depression or provides a passage between two points at a height above the ground, affording passage for pedestrians and vehicles.

drawbridge
At the entrance to fortifications, a bridge over the moat or ditch, hinged and provided with a raising and lowering mechanism so as to hinder or permit passage.

footbridge
A narrow structure designed to carry pedestrians only.

36

sidewalk bridge
A lightweight structural covering over a sidewalk to protect pedestrians from construction or cleaning of the structures overhead.

skywalk
A walkway that is located over the ground level and the street, and often connects buildings across a street.

Brise-soleil
A fixed or movable device, such as a fin or louver, designed to block the direct entrance of sun into a building.

Broach
A half pyramid above the corners of a square tower to provide a transition to an octagonal spire.

Broken arch See **Arch.**

Broken pediment See **Pediment.**

Broken rangework masonry See **Masonry**

Bronze See **Metal.**

Bronze Age
A period of human culture between the Stone Age and the Iron Age (4000–3000 B.C.), characterized by the use of bronze implements and weapons.

Brownstone See **Stone.**

Brutalism
An uncompromisingly modern style (1945–1960) which expresses itself in large scale using raw and exposed materials emphasizing stark forms. It was distinguished by its weighty textured surfaces and massiveness, created mainly by large areas of patterned concrete. Windows consist of tiny openings, and the combination of voids and solids gave walls an egg-crate appearance. Mechanical systems are left exposed on the interior of the bare structure.

Bucranium See **animal forms.**

Building
An enclosed and permanent structure for residential, commercial, industrial, institutional or office use, as distinguished from mobile structures or those not intended for occupancy.

Building adaptive reuse
To make suitable for a particular purpose or new requirements or conditions by means of modifications or changes to an existing building or structure.

Building addition
A floor or floors, room, wing or other expansion to an existing building; any new construction which increases the height or floor area of an existing building or adds to it in any fashion.

Building alteration
Construction in a building which changes the structural parts, equipment or location of openings without increasing the overall area or dimensions, as distinct from additions to an existing structure.

Building area
The total area of a site covered by buildings, as measured on a horizontal plane at ground level; terraces and uncovered porches are usually not included in this total.

Building artifact
An element in a building demonstrating human crafting, such as a stained-glass window or an ornament of archaeological or historic interest.

Building code
A collection of regulations by authorities having the jurisdiction to control the design and construction of buildings, alterations, repairs, quality of materials, use and occupancy; it contains minimum architectural, structural, and mechanical standards for sanitation, public health, safety, and welfare, and the provision of light and air.

Building component
An element manufactured as an independent unit, which can be joined with other elements, including electrical, fire protection, mechanical, plumbing, structural and other systems affecting health and safety.

Building conservation
The management of a building to prevent its decay, destruction, misuse, or neglect; may include a record of the history of the building and conservation measures applied.

Building construction
The fabrication and erection of a building by the process of assembly or by combining building components, subsystems, or systems.

Building environment
The combination of conditions that affect a person, piece of equipment or system in a building, such as lighting, noise, temperature and relative humidity.

Building grade
The ground elevation, established by a regulating authority, that determines the height of a building in a specific area.

Building height
The vertical distance measured from the grade level to a flat roof or to the average height of a pitched, gable, hip, or gambrel roof, not including bulkheads or penthouses.

Building inspector
A member of the building department who inspects construction to determine conformity to the building code and the approved plans, or one who inspects occupied buildings for violations of the building code.

Building line
A line or lines, established by law or agreement, usually parallel to the property lines, beyond which a structure may not extend; it usually does not apply to uncovered entrance platforms or terraces.

Building maintenance
Actions ensuring that a building remains in working conditions by preserving it from deterioration, decline, or failure.

Building material
Any material used in the construction of buildings, such as steel, concrete, brick, masonry, glass, and wood, among others.

Building permit
A written document that is granted by the municipal agency having jurisdiction, authorizing an applicant to proceed with construction of a specific project after the plans have been filed and reviewed.

Building preservation
The process of applying measures to maintain and sustain all of the existing materials, integrity, and form of a building including its structure and building artifacts.

Building reconstruction
The reproduction by new construction of the exact form and details of a building that no longer exists or artifacts as they once appeared.

Building rehabilitation
To restore a building to a useful life by repair, alteration or modification.

Building remodeling
To remake with a new structure, to reconstruct, or renovate.

Building renovation
To restore to an earlier condition, or improve by repairing or remodeling.

Building restoration
The process of returning a building as nearly as possible to its original form and condition, usually as it appeared at a particular time; may require removal of later work or reconstruction of work previously removed.

Building retrofit
The addition of new building materials, building elements, and other components not provided in the original construction to upgrade or change its functioning.

Building services
The utilities and services supplied and distributed within a building, including heating, air conditioning, lighting, water supply, drainage, gas and electric supply, fire protection and security protection.

Building subsystem
An assembly of components that performs a specific function in a building; for example, an air conditioning system consisting of its components, such as ductwork, a fan, air diffusers, and controls.

Bulkhead
A horizontal or inclined door over a stairway giving access to a cellar; a structure on the roof of a building covering a warter tank, shaft or service equipment.

Bull header bond See Bond.

Bull-nosed step See Step.

Bull stretcher bond See Bond.

Bungalow
A one-story frame house, or a summer cottage, often surrounded by a large covered veranda, widely bracketed gable roof; often built of rustic materials.

Bungalow style
This residential style (1890–1940), typified by a one-story house with gently pitched gables, had its roots in the Arts and Crafts movement. A lower gable usually covers a screen porch, which features battered piers at the corners. Rafters extend beyond the roof and are often exposed. Wood shingles are the favored exterior covering and are left natural. Windows are sash or casement with numerous lights.

Bush-hammered concrete
Concrete having an exposed aggregate finish, usually obtained with a power-operated bushhammer which removes the sand-cement matrix around the aggregate particles to a depth of 1/4".

Bush-hammered finish
A stone or concrete surface dressed with a bushhammer; used decoratively or to provide a roughened traction surface for treads, floors, and pavement.

Butt joint See Joint.

Butt splice See Splice.

Buttress
An exterior mass of masonry projecting from the wall to absorb the lateral thrusts from roof vaults; either unbroken in their height or broken into stages, with a successive reduction in their projection and width.

angle buttress
One of two buttresses that appear at right angles to each other, forming a corner support for a structure.

flying buttress
A characteristic feature of Gothic construction in which the lateral thrusts of a roof or vault are carried by a segmental masonry arch, usually sloping, to a solid pier or support sufficient to receive the thrust.

Byzantine architecture

The seat of the Roman Empire moved to Byzantium and a new style (300–1450) became the official architecture of the church. Plans were based on a Greek cross, with a large cupola rising from the center and smaller ones crowning the four small arms. The style was characterized by large pendentive supported domes, circular or horseshoe arches, elaborate columns, and richness in decorative elements. Doorways were square-headed with a semicircular arch over the flat lintel. The round arch, segmented dome, extensive use of marble veneer and rich frescoes with colored glass mosaics are also characteristic of this style. The most famous example is the Hagia Sophia in Istanbul.

Cc

Cabinet window See **Window.**

Cable molding See **Molding.**

Cabled fluting molding See **Molding.**

Calendar
A sculptured or painted emblematic series depicting the months of the year, often including the signs and symbols of the zodiac.

Calf's tongue molding See **Molding.**

Camber
A slight convex curvature intentionally built into a beam, girder, or truss to compensate for an anticipated deflection so that it will not sag under load; any curved surface to facilitate runoff of water.

Camber arch See **Arch.**

Camber beam See **Beam**

Camber window See **Window.**

Came
A slender rod of cast lead, with or without grooves, used in casements and stained-glass windows to hold the panes or pieces of glass together.

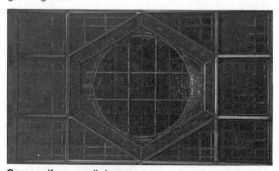

Campaniform capital See **Capital.**

Campanile
A bell tower detached from the main body of a church.

Canopy

Canal
A channel or groove as in the recessed portions of the face of a triglyph.

Canephora
An ornament representing a young maiden bearing a basket of ceremonial offerings on her head, used either as a column support or as a freestanding garden ornament.

Cant
A salient corner; a line or surface angled in relation to another, as in a wall sloped from perpendicular.

Canine   See **animal forms.**

Canopy
A decorative hood above a niche, pulpit, or stall; a covered area which extends from the wall of a building, protecting an enclosure.

41

Cant molding See Molding.

Cant wall See Wall.

Cant window See Window.

Cantilever
A structural member or any other element projecting beyond its supporting wall or column and weighted at one end or along its length to carry a proportionate weight on the projecting end.

Cantilevered
Refers to forms that have rigid structural members or walls projecting significantly beyond their vertical support.

Cantilevered step See Step.

Cap
The top member of any vertical architectural element; often projecting, with a drip for protection from the weather; the coping of a wall, the top of a pedestal or buttress, or the lintel of a door.

Cap molding See Molding.

Capital
The upper member of a column, pillar, pier or pilaster, crowning the shaft and usually decorated. It may carry an architrave, arcade or impost block. The classical orders each have representative capitals.

angle capital
A capital occurring at a corner column, especially an Ionic capital where the four volutes project equally on the diagonals, instead of along two parallel planes.

basket capital
A capital with interlaced bands resembling the weave of a basket, found in Byzantine architecture.

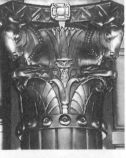

bifron capital
A capital with two fronts or faces looking in two directions, similar to a double herm.

bracket capital
A capital extended by brackets, lessening the clear span between posts, often seen in Near Eastern, Muslim, Indian, and some Spanish architecture.

campaniform capital
A bell shaped Egyptian capital representing an open papyrus profile.

composite capital
One of the five classical orders which combines acanthus leaves of the Corinthian order with the volutes of the Ionic order.

cushion capital
A capital resembling a cushion that is weighted down; in medieval architecture, a cubic capital with its lower angles rounded off.

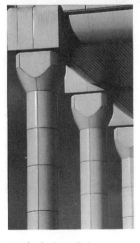

geminated capital
Coupled or dual capitals.

43

lotus capital
In ancient Egyptian architecture, a capital having the shape of a lotus bud.

palm capital
A type of Egyptian capital resembling the spreading crown of a palm tree; a column capital resembling the leaves of a palm tree.

papyriform capital
A capital of an Egyptian column with the form of a cluster of papyrus flowers.

quadrafron capital
Having four fronts or faces looking in four directions.

quadrafron capital

scalloped capital
A medieval block or cushion capital, when each lunette is developed into several truncated cones.

Carolingian architecture
The early Romanesque architecture (750–980) in France and Germany, based on an attempt by the Emperor Charlemagne to recreate Roman Imperial forms.

Carpenter Gothic style
A style (1800–1880) characterized by the application of Victorian Gothic motifs, often elaborate, by artisan woodworkers using modern machinery to produce ornamentation for building facades.

Carriage house
A building or part thereof for housing carriages or automobiles when they are not in use.

Carriage porch
A roofed structure over a driveway at the door to a building, protecting those entering or leaving or getting in or out of vehicles from the weather.

Cartoon See **Design drawing**.

Cartouche
A decorative ornamental tablet resembling a scroll of paper with the center either inscribed or left plain, but framed with an elaborate scroll-like carving.

Carved work
In stonework, any hand-cut ornamental features which cannot be applied from patterns.

Caryatid
A supporting member serving the function of a pier, column, or pilaster and carved and molded in the form of a draped, human figure; in Greek architecture, as in the Erectheum at the Acropolis in Athens.

Casement window See **Window**.

Casing
The exposed trim, flat or molded, molding, framing, or lining around a door or window; finished millwork, of uniform profile, which covers or encases a structural member, such as a post or beam. .

45

Castellated

Bearing the external fortification elements of a castle, in particular, battlements, turrets, crenellated patterns.

Castellation

A notched or indented parapet, originally used for fortifications, but afterwards used on church facades and intended as ornament.

Cast-in-place concrete See Concrete.

Cast iron See Metal.

Cast-iron facade

A load-bearing facade composed of prefabricated parts, commonly used on buildings around 1850-1870.

Cast-iron facade

Castle

A stronghold, building or group of buildings intended primarily to serve as a fortified post; a fortified residence of a nobleman.

Cast stone

A mixture of fine stone chips and Portland cement in a matrix. Once cast, it may be ground, polished or otherwise treated to simulate natural stone.

Catenary

The curve assumed by a flexible uniform cable suspended freely between two points. When uniformly loaded, the curve takes the form of a parabola.

Catenary arch See Arch.

Cathedral

The principal church of a diocese, which contains the home throne of a bishop, called the cathedra.

Caulking compound

A soft putty-like material intended for sealing joints in buildings, preventing leakage, or providing a seal at an expansion joint.

Cavetto molding See Arch.

Cavity wall See Wall.

Cavity wall masonry See Masonry.

Cavo-relievo See Relief.

Cedar See Wood.

Ceiling

The undercovering of a roof, or floor, generally concealing the structural members from the room or roof above, or the underside surface of vaulting. It may have a flat or curved surface, and may be self-supporting, suspended from the floor above, or supported from hidden or exposed beams.

suspended ceiling

A nonstructural ceiling suspended below the overhead structural slab or from the structural elements of a building and not bearing on the walls.

Ceiling joist   See Joist.

Cella
The sanctuary of a classical temple containing the cult statue of the god.

Cellar
That part of a building, the ceiling of which is entirely below grade; or having half or more of its clear height below grade.

Cellular construction
Construction with concrete elements in which part of the interior concrete is replaced by voids.

Cement
A material or a mixture of materials, without aggregate which, when in a plastic state, possesses adhesive and cohesive properties and hardens in place.

Cement plaster
Plaster with portland cement as the binder; sand and lime are added on the job before installation.

Centaur   See animal forms.

Center-hung door   See Door.

Centering
A temporary wooden framework placed under vaults and arches to sustain them while under construction; the form was covered with mortar so that the undersurface of the vault showed an impression of the boards that were used.

Center of vision   see Perspective projection

Centerpiece
An ornament placed in the middle of an area, such as a decoration in the center of a ceiling.

Central air-conditioning
An air conditioning system in which the air is treated by equipment at one or more central locations, and conveyed to and from these spaces by means of fans and pumps through ducts and pipes.

Central heating
A system in which heat is supplied to all areas of a building from a central plant through a network of ducts or pipes.

Centralized organization   See Organization.

Central visual axis   see Perspective projection

Ceramic mosaic tile   See Tile.

Ceramics
A hard, brittle, noncorrosive and nonconductive product made of clay or similar material, fired during its manufacture to produce porcelain, or terra-cotta.

Ceramic veneer
Architectural terra-cotta with ceramic vitreous or glazed surfaces, characterized by large face dimensions and their sections; the back is either scored or ribbed.

Chain molding   See Molding.

Chair rail
A horizontal wood strip, affixed to a plaster wall at a height which prevents the backs of chairs from damaging the wall surface.

Chaitya
A Buddhist or Hindu sanctuary, shrine, or temple.

Chalet
A timber house in the Alps, distinguished by exposed and decorative use of structural members, balconies, and stairs; the upper floors usually project beyond the story below.

Chamber
A room used for private living, conversation, consultation or deliberation, in contrast to more public and formal activities.

Chambranle
A structural feature, enclosing the sides and top of a doorway, window, fireplace or similar opening, often highly ornamental.

Chamfer

The groove or oblique surface made when an edge or corner is beveled or cut away, usually at a 45-degree angle to the adjacent faces.

Chamfer stop

Any ornamentation which terminates a chamfer.

Chamfered rustication

Rustication in which the smooth face of the stone parallel to the wall is deeply beveled at the joints so that, when the two meet, the chamfering forms an internal right angle.

Chancery

A building or suite of rooms designed to house any of the following; a low court with special functions, archives, a secretarial, a chancellery.

Channeling

A decorative groove in carpentry or masonry; a series of grooves in an architectural member, such as the flutes in a column.

Chaos

A state of utter disorder and confusion.

Chapel

A small area within a larger church, containing an altar and intended for private prayer; a small secondary church in a parish; a room designated for religious use within the complex of a school, college, or hospital.

Chapter house

A place for business meetings of a religious or fraternal organization; usually a building attached to a hall for gatherings; occasionally contains living quarters for members of such groups.

Charrette   See **Design.**

Chateau

A castle or imposing country residence of nobility in old France; any large country estate.

Chateau style

A style (1860–1898) characterized by massive and irregular, forms, steeply pitched hip or gable roofs with dormers, towers, and tall elaborately decorated chimneys with corbeled caps. Windows are paired and divided by a mullion and transom bar. Renaissance elements such as semicircular arches or pilasters are mixed with Tudor arches, stone window tracery, and Gothic finials.

Chattra

On top of a stupa, a stone umbrella which symbolizes dignity, composed of a stone disk on a vertical pole.

Chaumukh

In Indian architecture, four images, each facing a cardinal point, which are placed back-to-back.

Chavin style

A Peruvian style (900–200 B.C.) based on the worship of the jaguar god and characterized by grandiose terraced platforms constructed of stone, which were grouped around large sunken plazas, excellent stone sculpture, elaborate gold work, and remarkable ceremonies. The style is named after a town in central Peru, where a complex of massive stone buildings with subterranean galleries was surrounded by courtyards.

Checker

One of the squares in a checkered pattern, contrasted to its neighbor by color or texture; often only two effects are alternated, as in a chessboard.

Checkered

Those forms marked off with a pattern of checks or squares that is divided into different colors, or variegated by a checked or square pattern of different materials.

Checkerwork

In a wall or pavement, a pattern formed by laying masonry units so as to produce a checkerboard effect.

Cheek

A narrow upright face forming the end or side of an architectural or structural member or one side of an opening.

Cheneau

A gutter at the eaves of a building, especially one that is ornamental; an ornament, crest, or cornice.

Cherry See Wood.

Cherubs

A decorative sculpture or painting representing a chubby, usually naked infants; also called amorini or putti.

Cherubs

Chestnut See Wood.

Chevet

The rounded east end of a Gothic cathedral, including the apse and ambulatory.

Chevron

A symmetrical "V" shape that represents a triangle with its third side removed. It can be bordered, interlaced and repeated in various patterns pointing up or down, with an angle between 60 and 75 degrees.

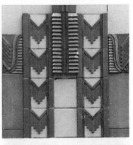

Chiaroscuro

The effect of light and shadow within an area or composition, brought about by the use of deep variations to enhance the forms.

Chicago School

A group of United states architects working in Chicago (1880-1910) active and known for major innovations in high-rise construction and for the development of modern commercial building design. The group included D.H. Burnham, J. W. Root, W. Le Baron. Jenney, W.B.Mundie, W. Holabird, and Louis Sullivan.

Chigi

A pair of crossed timbers which are placed at the end of the ridge of a roof of a Shinto shrine; also called forked finials.

Chimera   See animal forms.

Chimney

A vertical noncombustible structure containing one or more flues to carry smoke from the fireplaces to the outside, usually rising above the roof.

Chimney breast

A projection into a room of the fireplace walls that form the front portion of the chimney stack.

Chimney cap

A cornice forming a crowning termination of a chimney.

Chimney cricket

A small false roof built over the main roof behind a chimney, used to provide protection against water leakage where the chimney penetrates the roof.

Chimney hood

A covering which protects a chimney opening.

Chimney piece

An ornamental embellishment above or around the fire-place opening.

Chimney pot

A cylindrical pipe or brick, terra-cotta or metal, placed atop a chimney to extend it and thereby increase the draft.

Chimney stack

That part of a chimney which is carried above the roof of a building; a group of chimneys carried up together.

Chimu architecture

A style dominant in northern Peru (1150-1400) featured houses that were built in rows along symmetrically laid out streets inside high city walls. Buildings were constructed of adobe brick with wooden lintels. Walls were decorated with wide moldings with geometrical designs.

Ch'in architecture

A dynasty in China (221-206 B.C.), marked by the construction of the Great Wall of China.

Chinese architecture

A homogeneous traditional architecture (400-1600) repeated over the centuries in structures consisting of a wooden framework of columns and beams; stone and brick were used for permanent structures such as fortifications. The most prominent feature was tile-covered gabled roofs, with widely overhanging and upward curving eaves resting on complex multiple brackets. In pagodas each floor was articulated in a distinct rhythmical, horizontal effect.

Chip carving
Hand decoration of a wooden surface by slicing away chips, resulting in incised geometric patterns.

Chord
A principal member or pair of members of a truss extending from one end to the other, primarily to resist bending.

Church
An edifice or place of assemblage specifically set apart for Christian worship.

Churrigueresque style
A lavishly ornamented Spanish Baroque style (1700–1750) named after architect Jose Churriguera; the style was also adapted in South America.

Cincture
A ring of moldings around the top or bottom of the shaft of a column, separating the shaft from the capital or base; a fillet around a post.

Cinquefoil   See Tracery.

Cinqefoil arch   See Arch.

Circle
The simplest and most fundamental of all geometric shapes; a continuous curved line, every point of which is equidistant from a central point.

Circular arch   See Arch.

Circular stair   See Stair.

Citadel
A fortress or castle in or near a city; a refuge in case of a siege, or a place to keep prisoners.

Cityscape
Represented by the silhouette of groups of urban structures that make up a skyline, including distinguished landmarks as well as natural elements, such as rolling hills, mountains or large bodies of water.

Cladding
The process or the resulting product produced by the bonding of one metal to another, to protect the inner metal from weathering.

Clapboard siding   See Wood products.

Classical architecture
The architecture of Hellenic Greece and Imperial Rome on which the Italian Renaissance and subsequent styles were based. The five orders; the Doric, Ionic, Corinthian, Tuscan, and Composite are a characteristic feature.

Classical Revival style
An architectural movement based on the use of pure Roman and/or Greek forms, in reaction to Rococo and Baroque design.

Clathri
A lattice of bars as gratings for windows.

Clay tile See **Tile.**

Clerestory
An upper story or row of windows rising above the adjoining parts of the roof, designed to admit increased light into the inner space of the building.

Climax
A number of ideas so arranged that each succeeding one makes a stronger statement than its predecessor. The culmination or highest point is the summation of the whole process.

Clinic
A medical facility, independent or part of a hospital, in which ambulatory patients receive diagnostic and therapeutic medical and surgical care.

Clinker brick See **Brick.**

Clock
Any instrument for measuring or indicating time, especially a mechanical device with a numbered dial and moving hands or pointers.

Clock

Clocktower
Any instrument for measuring or indicating time, such as a mechanical device with a numbered dial and moving hands or pointers positioned in a single tower, or a tower-like portion of a structure.

Cloister
A square court surrounded by an open arcade, a covered walk around a courtyard, or the whole courtyard itself.

Cluster
Any configuration of elements that are grouped or gathered closely together.

Clustered column See **Column**.

Clustered organization See **Organization**.

Coach house
A building or part for housing carriages or automobiles when not in use; see carriage house.

Coat of arms
A tablet with a representation of a heraldic symbol.

Coffer
A recessed boxlike panel in a ceiling, soffit or vault; usually square, but often octagonal or lozenge shaped, sometimes dressed with simple moldings or elaborately ornamented.

Coffering
Ceiling with deeply recessed panels, often highly ornamental, executed in marble, brick, concrete, plaster, or stucco; a sunken panel in a vaulted ceiling.

Cogeneration
In a building, the on-site electric power generation utilizing both the electrical power and steam or hot water which is developed.

Cogged joint See **Joint**.

Coliseum
Any large Roman amphitheater; any large sports arena, open or roofed.

Collage See **Design drawing**.

Collar beam See **Beam**.

Collar brace
A structural member which reinforces a collar beam in medieval roof framing.

Collar joint
The joint between a roof structure and a collar beam.

Collar tie
In wood construction, a timber which prevents the roof framing from changing shape.

Colonial architecture
A classification pertaining to any architectural style that is transplanted from the motherland to overseas colonies. Examples are the Portuguese Colonial in Brazil, Dutch Colonial in New York, French Colonial in New Orleans, and English Colonial in all the North American colonies.

Colonial Revival style
The reuse of Georgian and Colonial design in the United States towards the end of the 19th and 20th centuries, typically in bank buildings, churches, and suburban homes.

Colonnade
A combination of columns placed at regular intervals, and arranged with regard to their structural or ornamental relationship to the building, usually on one side of a structure, aligned in a circular or straight pattern.

Colonette
A small column, usually decorative, found at the edge of windows; a thin round shaft to give a vertical line in elevation, or as an element in a compound pier.

Colonette

Color
The appearance of an object or surface, distinct from its form, shape, size, or position; depends on the spectral composition of incident light, spectral reflectance of the object, and spectral response of the observer.

Colored glass See Glass.

Column
A vertical structural com- pression member or shaft supporting a load which acts in the direction of its vertical axis and has both a base and a capital, designed to support an entablature or balcony.

angle column
A free-standing or engaged column placed at the outside corner of a building or portico.

angle column

banded column
A column or pilaster with drums alternately larger and smaller, alternately plainer and richer in decoration, or alternately protruding.

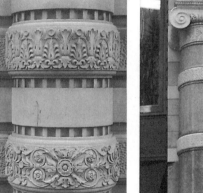

box column
A hollow, built-up column, constructed of wood, usually rectangular or square in section.

clustered column
A column or pillar composed of a cluster of attached or semi-attatched additional shafts, grouped together to act as a single structural or design element.

clustered columns

composite column
A column in which a metal structural member is completely encased in concrete containing special spiral reinforcement.

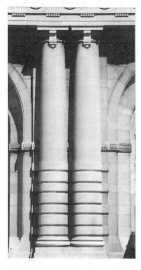

coupled column
Columns set as close pairs with a much wider space between the pairs.

diminished column
A column with a greater diameter at its base than at its capital.

engaged column
A column that is attached and appears to emerge from the wall, as decoration or as a structural buttress.

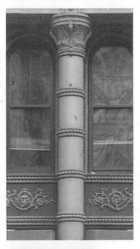

grouped columns
Three or more closely spaced columns or pilasters forming a group, often on one pedestal.

half-column
An engaged column projecting approximately one half its diameter, usually slightly more.

insulated column
A column which is entirely detached from a main building or structure.

Lally column
A proprietary name for a cylindrical column which is filled with concrete; used as a structural column to provide support to beams or girders.

mid-wall column
A column that carries a portion of a wall above it that is much thicker than its own diameter.

tension column
A column subjected to tensile stresses only.

wall column
A column which is embedded or partially embedded in a wall.

wreathed column
A column entwined by a band which presents a twisted or spiral appearance; a twisted column.

Column baseplate
A horizontal plate beneath the bottom of a column which transmits and distributes the column load to the supporting materials below the plate.

Columniation
A system in Classical architecture of grouping columns in a colonnade based on the diameters of the columns.

Commercial style
This term refers to the skeletal, rectangular style (1890–1915) of the first five- to fifteen- story skyscrapers, brought to full form in Chicago, New York, and Philadelphia. It was characterized by flat roofs and little ornament except for slight variations in the spacing of windows. Extensive use of glass was made possible by its steel-frame construction, which could bear the structural loads that masonry could not.

Common bond See **Bond**

Common brick See **Brick**

Complexity
Consisting of various parts united or connected together, formed by a combination of different elements; intricate, interconnecting parts that are not easily disentangled.

Compluvian
The opening in the center of the roof of the atrium in an ancient Roman house; it slopes inward to discharge rainwater into a cistern or tank in the center of the atrium.

Composite arch See **Arch**

Composite capital See **Capital**

Composite column See **Column**

Composite order
One of the five classical orders; a Roman elaboration of the Corinthian order; the acanthus leaves of its capitals are combined with the large volutes of the Ionic order and set on the diagonal in plan view.

Composition See **Design.**

Composition board
A building board fabricated of wood fibers in a binder, compressed under pressure at an elevated temperature.

Compound arch See **Arch.**

Computer-aided design
The analysis and/or design, modeling, simulation, or layout of building design with the aid of a computer.

Concave
Forms that are curved like the inner surface of a hollow sphere or circular arc.

Concave mortar joint See **Mortar joint.**

Concentric
Having a common center.

Conceptual architecture
A form of architecture (1960–1993) representing plans and drawings for buildings and cities never constructed, regarded as architecture arrested at the conceptual stage of development. The term also applied to work which could be realized but lacked the funds to construct it or work done as an end in itself. It was also defined as a limitless activity devoid of direction or dogma; that is, pure research or speculation.

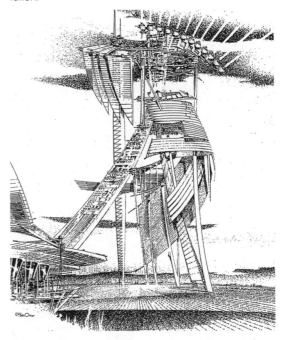

Conch
Semidome vaulting of an apse or eastern end of a church.

Concourse
An open space where several roads or paths meet; an open space for accommodating large crowds in a building, such as in a railway terminal or airport.

Conception See **Design.**

57

Concrete

A composite artificial building material consisting of an aggregate of broken stone mixed with sand, water and cement to bind the entire mass; fluid and plastic when wet and hard and strong when dry.

cast-in-place concrete

Concrete which is deposited in the place where it will harden as an integral part of the structure, as opposed to precast concrete.

precast concrete

Material that reduces the need for on-site formwork wherein precast panels are lifted into a vertical position and then attached to the structural frame.

prestressed concrete

A process of anchoring steel rods into the ends of forms, then stretching them before the concrete is poured, putting them under tension. When the concrete hardens, they spring back to their original shape, adding strength.

Concrete block

A hollow but sometimes solid concrete masonry unit, rectangular in shape, made from Portland cement and other aggregates.

decorative concrete block

A concrete masonry unit having special treatment of its exposed face for architectural effect; which may consist of exposed aggregates, or beveled recesses for patterned appearances when illuminated obliquely.

Concrete frame

A structure consisting of concrete beams, girders, and columns which are rigidly joined.

Concrete grille

An openwork barrier used to conceal, decorate, or protect an opening.

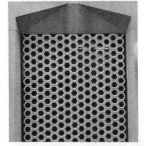

Concrete masonry   See Masonry.

Concrete panel

A panel that is precast and prefabricated elsewhere and placed in the structure rather than cast in place.

58

Concrete shell
A curved thin membrane which is usually poured or sprayed over forms with a network of steel rods and wire mesh; most often a lightweight aggregate is used to decrease the weight to strength ratio.

Condominium
An apartment house, office building or other multiple-unit complex; the units are individually owned, and there is joint ownership of common elements such as hallways, elevators, and all mechanical systems.

Configuration
The form of a figure as determined by the arrangement of its parts, outline, or contour.

Cone of vision see Perspective projection

Conical
Pertaining to a cone shape, generated by rotating a right triangle around one of its legs.

Conical dome See Dome.

Conical vault See Vault.

Conservatory
A school for teaching music, drama, or other fine arts; a glass-enclosed room of a house for the cultivation and display of plants.

Console
A vertical decorative bracket in the form of a scroll, usually higher than its projection from the wall to support a cornice, window, or a piece of sculpture.

Console table
A table attached to a wall and supported on consoles.

Construction
All the on-site work done in building or altering structures, from land clearance through completion, including excavation, erection and the assembly and installation of components and equipment.

Construction documents
The third phase of architectural basic services wherein the approved design development documents are used to prepare the working drawings, specifications and bidding information for approval by the owner.

Construction joint See Joint.

Construction management
The special management services performed by the architect or others during the construction phase of the project, either under a separate or special agreement with the owner.

Construction phase
The final phase of the architects basic services, which includes the architects general administration of the construction contract.

Constructivism
A movement (1920-1935) originating in Moscow based on order, logic, structure, abstraction and geometry, primarily in sculpture but with broad applications to architecture. An expression of construction was the base for all building design with emphasis on functional machine parts. Vladimir Tatlin's monument is the most notable example of this style. The industrial fantasies of Jacob Tchernikhov, published in 1933, show buildings perched on cantilevered structures, suggesting construction for construction's sake. The movement can be regarded as part of the broader movement of functionalism, with an accent on constructional expression. All traditional accessories, such as ornament and style, were discarded in favor of mass and space in relation to the sculptural forms.

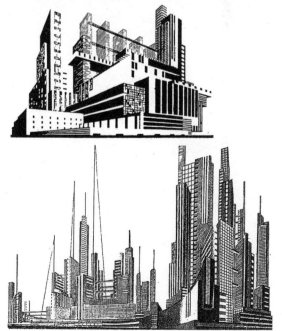

Consulate
A building where a consul conducts official business.

Contextual
Any doctrine emphasizing the importance of the context in establishing the meaning of terms, such as the setting into which a building is placed, its site, its natural environment, or its neighborhood.

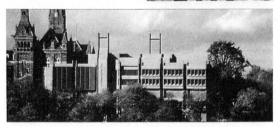

Contextualism
An approach to urban planning (1960–1970) that considers the city in its totality, the view that the experience of a city is greater than the sum of its parts. According to proponents, architecture must fit in, respond to, and mediate its surroundings.

Contour map
A topographic map which portrays relief by the use of contour lines which connect points of equal elevation; the closer the spacing of lines, the greater relative slope in that area.

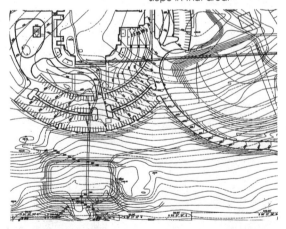

Contract documents
Those documents that comprise a contract, including plans and/or drawings, specifications; all addenda, modifications and changes, together with any other items stipulated as being specifically included.

Contractor
One who undertakes the performance of construction, providing labor and materials, in accordance with plans and specifications, and contracting for a specific cost and schedule for completion of the work.

Contrast
A juxtaposition of dissimilar elements to show the differences of form or color or to set in opposition in order to emphasize the differences.

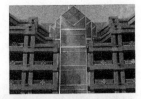

Control joint See **Joint.**

Convalescent home
A medical care institution for patients recovering from acute or postoperative conditions who do not require the skilled services provided by an extended-care facility, such as those services provided by a nursing home.

Convex
Forms that have a surface or boundary that curves outward, as in the exterior or outer surface of a sphere.

Cooling tower
A structure, usually located on the roof of a building, over which water is circulated, so as to cool it evaporatively by contact with air.

Cooperative apartment
A building of apartment units, owned and managed by a nonprofit corporation which sells shares in the building, entitling the shareholders to occupy apartments in the building.

Coping
A protective covering over the top course of a wall or parapet, either flat or sloping on the upper surface to throw off water. If it extends beyond the wall it may be cut with a drip to protect the wall below.

raking coping
A coping set on an inclined surface, as at a gable end.

Copper See Metal.

Coquillage
A representation of the forms of seashells as a decorative carving, and used over doors and windows, and in architraves and friezes.

Corbel

Corbel
A series of projections, each stepped progressively outward from the vertical face of a wall to support a cornice, or overhanging member; a projecting ornamental stone which supports a superincumbent weight.

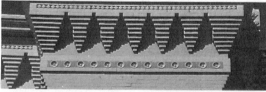

Corbel arch See Arch.

Corbel table
A raised band composed of small arches resting on corbels; projecting course of masonry supported on corbels near the top of a wall, such as a parapet or cornice.

Corbiestep

The stepped edge of an incline that terminates a masonry gable end wall, masking the surface of a pitched roof beyond; found in northern European masonry construction.

Corinthian order

The most ornamental of the three orders developed by the Greeks, characterized by a high base, pedestal, slender fluted shaft with fillets, ornate capitals using stylized acanthus leaves, and an elaborate cornice.

Corner

The position at which two lines or surfaces meet; the immediate exterior of the angle formed by the two lines or surfaces, as a corner of a building or structure. The corner is one of the most important zones expressing the junction of two facades. It can take many forms, such as recessed, rounded, retracted, framed or stepped in shape. It can be angular, curved, or articulated in many ways.

Corner

Corner bead molding See **Molding**

Corner board
A board which is used as trim on the external corner of a wood frame structure and against which the ends of the siding are fitted.

Cornerstone
A stone that is situated at a corner of a building uniting two intersecting walls, usually located near the base, and often carrying information about the structure.

Cornice
The uppermost division of an entablature; a projecting shelf along the top of a wall supported by a series of brackets; the exterior trim at the meeting of a roof and wall, consisting of soffit, fascia and crown molding.

boxed cornice
A hollow cornice, built up of boards and moldings, resulting in a soffit under the eaves.

horizontal cornice
The level cornice of the pediment under the two inclined cornices.

modillion cornice
A cornice supported by a series of modillions, often found in Composite and Corinthian orders.

open cornice
Overhanging eaves where the rafters are exposed at the eaves and can be seen from below.

raking cornice
A cornice following the slope of a gable, pediment, or roof.

Cornucopia ornament See **Ornament.**

Corona
The overhanging vertical member of a classical cornice supported by the bed moldings and crowned by the cymateum, usually incorporating a drip.

Corridor
A narrow passageway or gallery connecting several rooms or apartments within a residence, school, hospital, office building or other structure,

Corrosion
The deterioration of marble or concrete by a chemical reaction resulting from exposure to weathering, moisture, chemicals, or other agents in the environment in which it is placed.

Corrugated
Shaped into folds of parallel and alternating ridges and valleys, either to provide additional strength, or to vary the surface pattern.

Corrugated metal
Sheet metal which has been drawn or rolled into parallel ridges and furrows to provide additional mechanical strength; aluminum and galvanized sheet metal are the most widely used.

Cortile
An interior courtyard enclosed by the walls of a palace or other large building.

Cottage
A small rustic country house of the late 18th century.

Counterpoint
A contrasting but parallel element or theme.

interweaving counterpoint
The forms or elements are integrated, with each one being a part of the other.

overlapping counterpoint
The forms are in contact but are not connected to each other.

parallel counterpoint
The ideas run together, but do not cross or interweave, as in bands running in the same direction.

Coupled column See Column.

Coupled window See Window.

Course
A layer of masonry units running horizontally in a wall or over an arch that is bonded with mortar. The horizontal joints run the entire length; the vertical joints are broken so that no two form a continuous line.

Coursed ashlar masonry See Masonry.

Coursed masonry See Masonry.

Coursed rubble See Masonry.

Court
An open space about which a building or several buildings are grouped, completely or partially enclosing the space. They may be roofed over with glass or open to the air.

Courtyard
An open area within the confines of other structures, sometimes as a semipublic space.

Coussinet
The stone which is placed on the impost of a pier to receive the first stone of an arch.

Cove ceiling
A ceiling having a cove at the wall line or elsewhere.

Cove molding See Molding.

Cover molding See Molding.

Crane
A piece of construction machinery containing a mechanical device for lifting or lowering a load and moving it horizontally, in which the hoisting mechanism is an integral part of the boom.

Crenel
The open space between the members of a battlement, producing a pattern of repeated and identical indentations.

Crenelet
A small crenel, used as a decorative design.

Crenellated molding See Molding

Crenellation
A pattern of repeated depressed openings in a fortification parapet wall.

Crespidoma
The solid mass of masonry at the base forming the stepped platform upon which a classical temple is constructed.

Crescent
A building or series of buildings on a street whose facades are of a unified architectural scheme and follow a concave arc of a circle or ellipse in plan.

Crescent arch See Arch.

Crest
An ornament on a roof, a roof screen or wall which is frequently perforated, and consists of rhythmic and identical patterns that are highly decorative.

Crest tile See Tile.

Cripple window See Window.

Crocket capital See Capital.

Crocket ornament See Ornament.

Cross
Two lines intersecting each other at right angles so that the four arms are of equal length.

Cross bracing See **Brace**.

Cross vault See **Vault**.

Crossbeam See **Beam**.

Crossette
A lateral projection of the architrave moldings of classical doors and windows at the extremities of the lintel or head; a small projecting part of an arch stone, which hangs upon an adjacent stone.

Crown
Any uppermost or terminal features in architecture; the top of an arch including the keystone; the corona of a cornice, often including the elements above it.

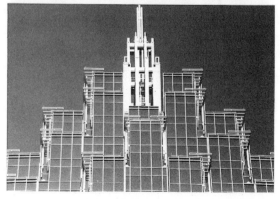

Crown molding See **Molding**.

Crowstone
The top stone of the stepped edge of a gable.

Cruciform
The characteristic cross-shaped plan for Gothic and other large churches that is formed by the intersection of nave, chancel, and apse with the transepts.

Crypt
A story in a church below or partly below ground level and under the main floor, often containing chapels and sometimes tombs; a hidden subterranean chamber or complex of chambers and passages.

Crypta
In ancient Roman architecture, a long, narrow vault sometimes below ground level, for the storage of grain.

Crystalline
A three-dimensional structure consisting of periodically repeated, identically constituted, congruent unit cells; found abundantly in natural objects.

Cul-de-sac
A street, lane, or alley that is closed at one end, usually having an enlarged, somewhat circular area for turning around.

Cunieform
Designs having a wedge-shaped form; especially applied to characters, or to the inscriptions in such characters, of the ancient Mesopotamians and Persians.

Cupola
A towerlike device rising from the roof, usually terminating in a miniature dome or turret with a lantern or windows to let light in.

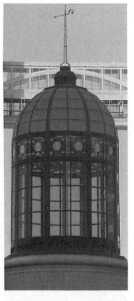

Curb roof See Roof.

Curtail
A spiral scroll-like termination of any architectural member, as at the end of a stair rail.

Curtail step See Step.

Curtain wall See Wall.

Curvilinear
Forms that are bounded by or characterized by curved lines, whether geometric or free-flowing.

Cushion capital See Capital.

Cusp
The intersection of two arcs or foliations in a tracery; the figure formed by the intersection of tracery arcs or foliations.

Cusped arch See Arch.

Cuspidation
Any system of ornamentation which consists of or contains cusps.

Cutaway see Projection drawing

Cut stone
Any stone cut or machined to a specified size and shape to conform to drawings, for installation in a designated place; it can also be carved by the intaglio method.

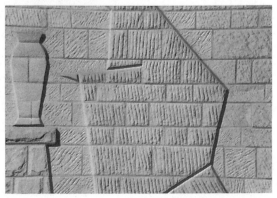

Cyclopean masonry See Masonry.

Cylindrical
Having the shape of a cylinder, generated by rotating a rectangle around one of its sides.

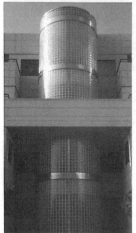

Cyma molding See Molding.

Cyma recta molding See Molding.

Cyma reversa molding See Molding.

Cymatium molding See Molding.

Cypress See Wood.

D·d

Dado
The middle portion of a pedestal between the base and the surface. A rectangular groove cut across the full width of a piece of wood to receive the end of another piece.

Dagoba
In Buddhist architecture, a monumental structure containing relics of Buddha or a Buddhist saint.

Daubing See Plaster.

De Stijl movement
A movement (1892–1921) which began in Holland with two branches of the avant-garde; the Purists and the Expressionists. Its name came from the magazine which published their manifestos. Influenced by Cubist painting, right angles and smooth walls were the order of the day. The cube served as the point of departure as an elementary expression of space into which the internal walls continued.

Decastyle
A building having a portico or row of ten columns.

Deck
The flooring of a building or other structure; a flat open platform, as on a roof.

Deconstructivism
An architectural style (1984–) known as "neo-modernism," or "post-structuralism." It takes many of its forms from the work of the Constructivists of the 1920s, such as Chernikhov and Leonidou. It takes modernist abstraction to an extreme and exaggerates already known motifs. It is an antisocial architecture, based on intellectual abstraction. Some of its proponents are Bernard Tschumi and his design for the Parc de la Villette, Paris; Peter Eisenman's Wexner Center for the Visual Arts, Ohio; and work by Frank Gehry, Architectonica, SITE, and Morphosis.

Decor
The combination of materials, furnishings, and objects used in interior decoration to create an atmosphere or style.

Decorated style
The second of three phases of English Gothic (1280–1350) was characterized by rich decoration and geometric tracery and by the use of multiple ribs in the vaulting. The early development was geometric, while the later forms were curvilinear, with complicated rib vaulting and naturalistic carved foliage displaying a refinement of stonecutting techniques.

Decorative glass See **Glass.**

Deflection
The deformation or displacement of a structural member as a result of loads acting on it.

Dentil
A series of closely spaced ornamental rectangular blocks resembling teeth, used as moldings most often in continuous bands just below the cornice.

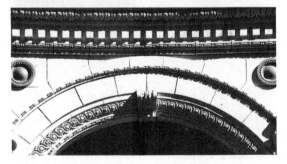

Dentil band
A plain, uncarved band occupying the position in a cornice where dentils would normally occur.

Depressed arch See **Arch.**

Depression Modern style
Designs from the decade of economic depression (1935–1945) are represented in this style, which marked a reaction against the Art Deco style. It was characterized by simplicity, smoothness of forms, clarity of line, horizontality, streamlining and functional expressiveness. .

Depth
The extent, measurement or distance from top to bottom (downwards), or from front to back (inwards), or an element consisting of several layers.

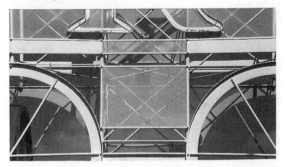

Design
To compose a plan for a building; the architectural concept of a building as represented by plans, elevations, renderings, and other drawings; any visual concept of a man-made object, as of a work of art.

charrette
The intense effort to complete an academic architectural problem within a specified time; from the French word meaning "cart;" used to carry student work at the Ecole des Beaux Arts to be judged.

composition
The forming by a combination of various elements into proper position to form a whole in terms of the structure or in the organization.

conception
A drawing of something that does not yet exist.

image
Any representation of form or features, but especially one of the entire figure of a person; a statue, effigy, bust, relief, intaglio.

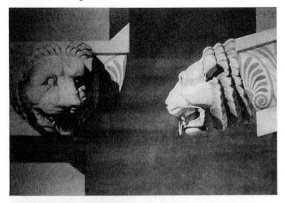

isometric drawing
A three-dimensional projection in which all planes are drawn parallel to the corresponding axes at true dimensions; horizontals are at 30 degrees from the normal horizontal axis; verticals are parallel to the vertical axis.

mock-up
A model of an object in the course of design, as in a cross-section of a window or its parts; built to scale or full size, for studying construction details, judging appearance, and/or testing performance.

model
A representation or reproduction, usually at a small scale, for purposes of study or to illustrate construction.

parti
A scheme or concept for the design of a building, represented by a diagram.

perspective drawing
A graphic representation of a project or portion thereof as it would appear in three dimensions.

preliminary drawing
Drawings prepared during the early stages of the design stages of a project.

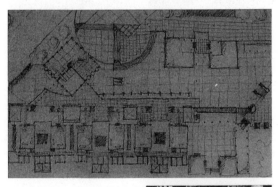

presentation drawing
Any of a set of design drawings made to articulate and communicate a design concept or proposal, as for exhibition, review, or publication.

Design development

The second phase of the architect's basic services; describing the character of the project as to structural, mechanical, and electrical systems, materials and all other essentials, and probable construction costs.

Design drawing

Any of the drawings made to aid in the visualization, exploration, and evaluation of a concept in the design process.

cartoon

A drawing or painting made as a detailed model of an architectural embellishment, often full-scale, to be transferred in preparation for a fresco, mosaic or tapestry.

collage

An artistic composition of often diverse materials and objects, in unlikely or unexpected juxtaposition, which are pasted over a surface, often with unifying lines and color.

detail

A small or secondary part of a painting, statue, building, or other work of art, especially when considered or represented in isolation.

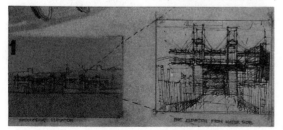

diagram

A plan, sketch, drawing, chart or graph, not necessarily representational, that explains, demonstrates or clarifies the arrangement and relationship of the parts to a whole.

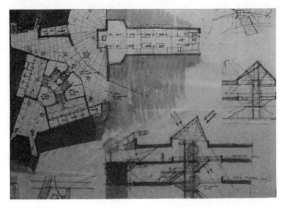

draft

A preliminary sketch of a design or plan, especially one executed with the idea of potential revision or refinement.

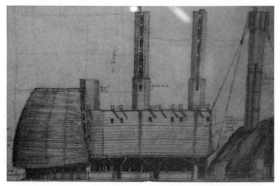

esquisse

A first sketch or very rough design drawing showing the concepts or general features of a project.

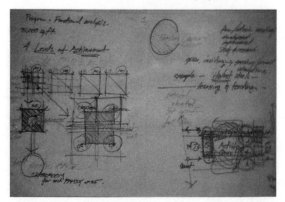

rendering
A drawing, especially a perspective of a building or interior space, artistically delineating materials, shades and shadows; done for the purpose of presentation and persuasion.

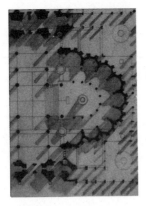

scheme
The basic arrangement of an architectural composition. Preliminary sketch for a design.

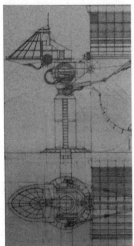

study
A drawing executed as an educational exercise, produced as a preliminary to a final work, or made to record observations.

vignette
A drawing that is shaded off gradually into the surrounding paper so as to leave no definite line at the border.

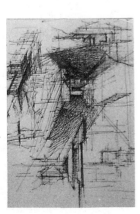

Detail See **Design drawing.**

Diaglyph See **Relief.**

Diagonal
Joins two nonadjacent sides of a polygon, with a slanted or oblique direction from one corner to the other; their use in a square or rectangle produces two triangular shapes.

Diagonal bond See **Bond.**

Diagonal brace See **Brace.**

Diagonal sheathing
A covering of wood boards placed over exterior studding at a diagonal with respect to the vertical; provides a base for the application of wall cladding.

Diagram See **Design drawing.**

Diamond fret
A molding that is usually continuous, consisting of fillets that intersect to form a diamond shape, or rhombus.

Diamondwork masonry See **Masonry.**

Diaper patterns
Flat patterns based on grids, containing either straight or curved lines; the grid may overlap or produce figures by connecting the diagonals and by combining them with circles, arcs and segments.

Dimetric projection see **Projection drawing**

Diminished arch See **Arch.**

Diorama
A large painting, or series of paintings, intended for exhibition in a darkened room in a manner that produces an appearance of reality created by optical illusions; a building in which such paintings are exhibited.

71 **Discharging arch** See **Arch.**

Discontinuous construction
Construction where there is no solid connection between the rooms of a building and the structure; or between one section and another; used to prevent the transmission of sound along a solid path.

Dogtooth bond See Bond.

Dolomite See Stone.

Dome
A curved roof structure that spans an area on a circular base, producing an equal thrust in all directions. A cross-section of the dome can be semicircular, pointed or segmented.

bell-shaped dome
A dome whose cross-section is shaped in the form of a bell.

geodesic dome
Consisting of a multiplicity of similar straight linear elements, arranged in triangles or pentagons, the members in tension having a minimal cross section, and making up a spherical surface usually in the shape of a dome.

interdome
The space between the inner and outer shells of a dome.

lattice dome
A steel dome structure having members which follow the circles of latitude, and two sets of diagonals replacing the lines of longitude and forming a series of isosceles triangles.

lattice dome

melon dome
A melonlike ribbed dome, either interior or exterior.

onion dome
In Russian Orthodox church architecture, a bulbous dome which terminates in a point and serves as a roof structure over a cupola or tower.

radial dome
A dome built with steel or timber trusses arranged in a radial manner and connected by polygonal rings at various heights.

saucer dome
A dome whose rise is much smaller than its radius.

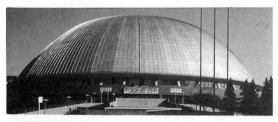

semicircular dome
A dome in the shape of a half sphere.

semidome
A dome equivalent to one-quarter of a hollow sphere, covering a semicircular area, such as an apse.

Dominance
Occupying a preeminent or influential position; forms exercising the most influence or governing control.

Door
A hinged, sliding, tilting, or folding panel for closing openings in a wall or at entrances to buildings, rooms, or cabinets and closets.

Door buck
A metal or wood surface, set in a wall, to which the finished frame is attached.

Door casing
The finished frame surrounding a door; the visible frame.

Doorframe
An assembly built into a wall consisting of two upright members (jambs) and a head *lintel) over the doorway; encloses the doorway and provides support on which to hang the door.

Door head
The uppermost member of a door frame; a horizontal projection above a door.

Door jamb
The vertical member on each side of a door.

Doorknocker
A knob, bar, or ring of metal, attached to the outside of an exterior door to enable a person to announce his or her presence, usually held by a hinge so that it can be lifted to strike a metal plare.

Door mullion
The center vertical member of a double-door opening set between two single active leaves, usually the strike side of each leaf.

Door muntin
An intermediate vertical member that divides the panels of a door.

Door panel
A distinct section or division of a door, recessed below or raised above the general level, or one enclosed by a frame.

Door rail
A horizontal cross member connecting the hinge stile to the lock stile, both at the top and bottom of the door and at intermediate locations, may be exposed as in panel doors, or concealed, as in flush doors.

Door sill
The horizontal member, usually a board, covering the floor joint on the threshold of a door.

Door stile
One of the upright structural members of the frame at the outer edge of a door.

Doorstop
A strip against which a door shuts in its frame; a device placed on a wall behind a door, or mounted on the floor, to prevent the door from opening too wide.

Door surround
An ornamental border encircling the sides and top of a door frame.

Door threshold
A strip fastened to the floor beneath a door, usually required to cover the joint where two types of floor material meet; may provide weather protection at exterior doors.

Door transom
A crossbar separating a door from a light or window located above it.

Door types

accordion door
A hinged door consisting of a system of panels hung from an overhead track, folding back like the bellows of an accordion; when open the panels close flat; when closed, the panels interlock with each other.

acoustical door
A door having a sound-deadening core, gasketed stops along the top and sides, and an automatic drop seal along the bottom, especially constructed to reduce noise transmission through it.

aluminum door
Used for storefront entrances, due to high corrosion resistance.

bi-fold door
A folding door that divides into two parts, the inner leaf of each part being hung from an overhead track, and the outer leaf hinged at the jamb.

blank door
A recess in a wall, having the appearance of a door; usually used for symmetry of design; any door which has been sealed off but is still visible on the surface.

blind door
The representation of a door, inserted to complete a series of doors, or to give symmetry.

center-hung door
A door which is supported by and swings on a pivot recessed in the floor at a point located on the center line of the door's thickness; may be either single-swing or double-acting.

dutch door
A door consisting of two separate leaves, one above the other; the leaves may operate independently or together.

flush door
Plain and unadorned, inset with panels of textured glass.

flush paneled door
A paneled door in which, on one or both faces, the panels are finished flush with the rails and stiles.

folding door
One of two or more doors which are hinged together so that they can open and fold in a confined space.

french door
A door having a top rail, bottom rail, and stiles, which has glass panes throughout its entire length; often used in pairs.

glass door
A door consisting of heat-strengthened or tempered glass, with or without rails or stiles; used primarily as an entrance door, especially for retail stores.

hollow-core door
A wood flush door having a framework of stiles and rails encasing a honeycombed core of corrugated fiberboard, or a grid of interlocking horizontal and vertical wood strips.

interior door
Usually hollow-core or solid-core made to be soundproof.

louvered door
A door having a louvered opening, usually with horizontal blades, that allows for the passage or circulation of air while the door is closed.

metal-clad door
A flush door having face sheets of light-gauge steel bonded to a steel channel frame, or a door having a structural wood core clad with galvanized sheet metal.

overhead door
A door of either the swing-up or the roll-up type, constructed of one or several leaves; when open, it assumes a horizontal position above the door opening.

paneled door
A door having a framework of stiles, rails, and muntins which form one or more frames around thinner recessed panels.

pivoted door
A door hung on center or offset pivots as distinguished from one hung on hinges or a sliding mechanism.

pocket door
A door that slides in and out of a recess in a doorway wall; requiring no room for the door swing.

revolving door
An exterior entrance door consisting of four leaves at right angles to each other, set in the form of a cross, which pivot about a common vertical axis within a cylindrical-shaped vestibule.

rolling door
A large door consisting of horizontal, interlocking metal slats guided by a track on either side, opening by coiling about an overhead drum at the head of the door opening.

roll-up door
A door made of small horizontal interlocking metal slats which are guided in a track; the configuration coils around an overhead drum which is housed at the head; may be manually or electrically operated.

sliding door
A door that is mounted on a track, which slides in a horizontal direction parallel to the wall on which it is mounted.

solid-core door
A wood flush door having a solid core of lumber, particle board, or one consisting of mineral composition.

swinging door
A door that turns on hinges or pivots about a vertical edge when opened.

tempered glass door
Common for commercial use.

venetian door
A door having a long narrow window at each side similar in form to that of a venetian window, or a Palladian door.

wood door
Either solid or hollow with veneer, exterior doors are coated with waterproof adhesives.

Doorway
The framework in which the door hangs, or the entrance to a building; the key area of interest in a facade as a natural focal point and design element giving human scale, and containing the street number.

Doric order
The first and simplest of the orders, developed by the Dorian Greeks, consisting of relatively short shafts with flutes meeting with a sharp arris, simple undecorated capital, square abacus, and having no base. The entablature consists of a plain architrave, a frieze of triglyphs and metopes, and a cornice. The corona contained mutules in the soffit.

Dormer
A structure projecting from a sloping roof usually housing a vertical window that is placed in a small gable, or containing a ventilating louver.

dormer cheek
The vertical sides of a dormer.

eyebrow dormer
A low dormer on the slope of a roof, having no sides, the roofing being carried over it in a wavy line.

shed dormer
A dormer whose eave line is parallel to the eave of the main roof, as opposed to one whose eave is gabled.

Dormer window See **Window.**

Dormitory
A multi-occupancy building which contains a series of sleeping rooms, bathrooms, and common areas.

Double-sunk
Recessed or lowered in two steps, as when a panel is sunk below the surface of a larger panel.

Double-hung window See **Window.**

Double vault See **Vault**

Double window See **Window.**

Douglas fir See **Wood.**

Dovetail joint See **Joint.**

Dovetail molding See **Molding.**

Downspout
A vertical pipe that carries water from the roof gutters to the ground or cistern.

Draft See **Design drawing**

Drafted margin
A narrow dressed border around the face of a stone, usually about the width of a chisel edge.

Drawbridge See **Bridge.**

Dressed lumber
Lumber having one or more of its faces planed smooth.

Dressed stone
Stone that has been worked to a desired shape; the faces to be exposed are smooth, usually ready for installation.

Dressing
Masonry and moldings of better quality than the facing materials, used around door and window openings or at corners of buildings.

Drip cap
A horizontal molding fixed to a door or window frame to divert the water from the top rail, causing it to drip beyond the outside of the frame.

Drip molding See **Molding.**

Dripstone cap
A continuous horizontal drip molding on a masonry wall.

Dripstone course
A continuous horizontal drip molding on a masonry wall.

Drop
Any one of the guttae attached to the underside of the mutules or triglyphs of a Doric entablature.

Drop arch See **Arch.**

Drop molding See **Molding.**

Drum
A cylindrical or polygonal wall below a dome, often pierced with windows.

Dry masonry
Masonry laid without mortar.

Drywall
An interior wall, constructed with a material such as gypsum board or plywood; usually supplied in large sheets or panels, that do not require water to apply.

Duct
A nonmetallic or metallic tube for housing wires or cables; may be underground or embedded in concrete floor slabs; a duct usually fabricated of metal, used to transfer air from one location to another.

Ductwork
The ducts in a heating, ventilating or air conditioning system.

Dumbbell tenement
A five- to seven-story multiple dwelling unit in urban areas, characterized by a long, narrow plan with an indentation on each side, forming a shaft for light and air, hence its resemblance in plan to a dumbbell.

Duplex
A house having a separate apartment for two families, especially a two-story house having two separate entrances and a complete apartment on each floor; an apartment with rooms on two connected floors.

Dutch bond   See **Bond.**

Dutch Colonial style
A style adopted by the Dutch settlers in New York and New Jersey (1650–1700), characterized by the use of brick and stone walls with gambrel or double-pitched roofs and flared lower eaves which extend beyond the front and rear walls, forming a deep overhang.

Dutch door   See **Door.**

Dutch gable   See **Gable.**

E·e

Early Christian architecture
The final phase of Roman architecture (200–1025) was influenced by the adoption of Christianity as the state religion and the rise of the Byzantine style. The Roman basilica form was adopted as the ground plan for most early Christian churches. These simple rectangular plans consisted of a nave with two side aisles and a longitudinal and horizontal emphasis.

Early English architecture
The first English Gothic style (1200–1250) to follow the Norman style featured molding, consisting of rounds and deep hollows, which produced a strong effect of light and shadow. Arches were lancet-shaped; doorways were deeply recessed with numerous moldings in the arch and jambs. Windows are long and narrow, and almost always pointed. Pillars consist of small shafts arranged around a larger central pier.

Eastern Stick Style
An American residential style (1855–1900) characterized by exposed framing overlaid on clapboard in horizontal, vertical or diagonal patterns to suggest the frame structure underneath. Steeply pitched gable roofs, cross gables, towers and pointed dormers, and porches and verandas are also characteristic. Oversized corner posts, purlins, brackets, and railings complement decorative woodwork produced by the stickwork.

Eastlake style
A style (1870–1880) characterized by a massive quality, in which posts, railings and balusters were turned on a mechanical lathe. Large curved brackets, scrolls and other stylized elements are placed at every corner or projection along the facade. Perforated gables, carved panels and a profusion of spindles and latticework along porch eaves are typical. Lighter elements are combined with oversized members to exaggerate the three-dimensional facade..

Eave
The projecting overhang at the lower edge of a roof that sheds rain water.

Eaves channel
A channel or small gutter along the top of a wall; it conveys the roof rainwater to downspouts or discharges it through gargoyles.

Ebony See Wood.

Eccentric
Not having the same center or center line; departing or deviating from the conventional or established norm, or model.

Echinus
The convex projecting molding of eccentric curve supporting the abacus of the Doric capital.

Eclectic Style
The selection of elements from diverse styles for architectural decorative designs, particularly during the late 19th century in Europe and America.

Ecological architecture
A style of architecture (1970–) developed In response to the problems of expensive fuels and other environmental factors. Various projects were undertaken to construct self-sufficient, self-serving buildings that are independent of public utilities by exploiting ambient energy sources such as wind power, solar radiation, and recycling techniques.

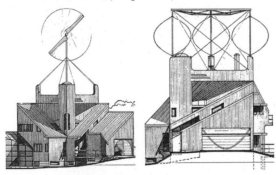

Efflorescence
An encrustation of soluble salts, commonly white, deposited on the surfaces of stone, brick, plaster, or mortar; usually caused by free alkalies leached from mortar or adjacent concrete as moisture moves through it.

Egg and dart molding See Molding.

Egyptian architecture
An ancient architecture along the Nile River from Neolithic times (3000 B.C–200 A.D.), built of reed huts with inward sloping walls and thick bases to resist the annual inundation. The decorative "bundling" of reeds later influenced stone construction of fluted columns and capitals. Massive funerary monuments and temples were built of stone using post-and-lintel construction, with closely spaced columns carrying the stone lintels, supporting a flat roof. A hypostyle hall, crowded with columns, received light from clerestories above. Walls were carved in ornamental hieroglyphs in low relief. There were many varieties of columns, often used side by side, their capitals distinctly ornate, based on the lotus, papyrus, or palm.

Egyptian cornice
The characteristic cornice of most Egyptian buildings, consisting of a large cavetto decorated with vertical leaves and a roll molding below.

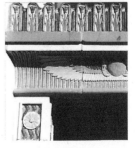

Egyptian Revival style

A revival style (1830–1850) distinguished by distinctive columns and capitals and a smooth monolithic exterior finish. Characteristic battered walls are edged with roll moldings, tall straight-headed windows with splayed jambs, and a deep cavetto or gorge-and-roll cornice. Roofs are flat, and the smooth wall surface lends a monumental appearance reminiscent of pylons or gateways to Egyptian temples.

Elastomeric

Any material having the properties of being able to return to its original shape after being stressed; such as a roofing material which can expand and contract without rupture.

Elevation

A drawing showing the vertical elements of a building, either interior or exterior, as a direct projection to a vertical plane.

Elevation

Elevator

A platform or enclosure that is stabilized by guiderails, and can be raised or lowered in a vertical shaft for transporting people or freight from one level of a structure to another.

Elgin Marbles

A collection of sculptures, taken from the Parthenon in Athens by Lord Elgin; preserved in the British Museum since 1816. The finest surviving work of Greek sculptural decoration of the classical age; the collection includes a number of metopes, fragments of pediment statues, and an extended series of blocks carved in low relief of the cella frieze.

Elizabethan style

A transitional style between the Gothic and Renaissance in England (1558–1603), named after the queen, consisting mostly of designs for country houses, characterized by large windows and by strap iron ornamentation.

Elliptical

A plane figure resembling an ellipse, whose radius of curvature is continually changing; a three-centered arch is an example of a construction to an elliptical curve.

Elliptical arch See Arch.

Elm See wood.

El Tajin Style
A style of Mesoamerican architecture (200–900 A.D.) as seen at the Pyramid of Niches, El Tajin, the Totonac capital in Vera Cruz, Mexico, characterized by elaborately carved recessed niches in planes of geometric ornamentation.

Embattlements
Having battlements; a crenelated molding.

Embedded organization See Organization.

Embellishment
Ornamentation; adornment with decorative elements.

Emboss
To raise or indent a pattern on the surface of a material; sometimes produced by the use of patterned rollers.

Embrasure
The crenels or spaces between the merlons of a battlement; an enlargement of a door or window opening at the inside face of a wall by means of splayed sides.

Emphasis
A special importance or significance placed upon or imparted to an element or form by means of contrast or counterpoint; a sharpness or vividness of outline.

Empire style
The elaborate neoclassic style (1800–1830) of the French Empire in the wake of Napoleon, characterized by the use of delicate but elaborate ornamentation, imitated from Greek and Roman examples, and by the use of military and Egyptian motifs.

Encarpus
A sculptural festoon of fruit and flowers.

Encaustic tile See Tile.

Engaged column See Column.

Engineer
A person trained and experienced in the profession of engineering; one licensed to practice the profession by the authority in the area.

Enriched
Having embellishments.

English bond See Bond.

English cross bond See Bond.

Entablature
The superstructure composed of an architrave immediately above the columns, central frieze, and upper projecting cornice, consisting of a series of moldings. The proportions and detailing are different for each order, and strictly prescribed.

Entasis
Intentional slight curvature given to the vertical profile of a tapered column to correct the optical illusion that it appears thinner in the middle if the sides are left straight.

Entrance
Any passage that affords entry into a building; an exterior door, vestibule or lobby.

Envelope
The imaginary shape of a building indicating its maximum volume; used primarily to check the plan, setback, and similar restrictions regarding zoning regulations.

Envelope forms
With curtain-wall systems, the actual construction and arrangement of the surfaces enclosing the building are totally independent of the bearing system.

Environment
The combination of all external conditions which may influence, modify, or affect the actions of a person, piece of equipment, or any system.

Environmental design
The professions collectively responsible for the design of man's physical environment, including architecture, engineering, landscape architecture, urban planning and similar environment-related professions.

Environmental impact statement
A detailed analysis of the probable environmental consequences of proposed federal legislation, or large-scale construction making use of federal funds, likely to have significant effects on environmental quality.

Equilateral arch   See **Arch.**

Equilibrium
The state of a body in which the forces acting on it are equally balanced.

Erection
The hoisting and installing in place of the structural components of a building, using a crane, hoist, or any other power system.

Erection bracing
Bracing which is installed during erection to hold the framework in a safe condition until sufficient permanent construction is in place to provide full stability.

Ersatz style
A German word meaning "substitute" or "replacement," used by architectural critic Charles Jencks to describe architecture (1973–1975) with forms borrowed indiscriminately from various sources. This is partly the result of modern technology, which is capable of producing architecture in any style. It can also be considered as any "pastiche" which captures the essence of the original.

Escalator
A moving power-driven stairway consisting of steps attached to an inclined continuously moving belt for transporting passengers up or down between the floors in a structure.

Escutcheon
A protective plate surrounding the keyhole of a door or door handle.

Escutcheon pin
A small nail, usually brass, for fixing an escutcheon, often ornamental.

Esquisse   See **Design drawing**

Etruscan architecture
A style (700–280 B.C.) which flourished in western central Italy until the Roman conquest; it is largely lost, except for underground tombs and city walls, but the characteristic true stone arch influenced later Roman construction methods. Examples that survive show forms that were rich in ornamentation.

Eurhythmy
Harmony, orderliness, and elegance of proportions.

Evolutionary architecture
This style is defined by its major proponent, Eugene Tsui, as design that grows and develops based on climatic and ecological elements, as well as advances in science and technology. The design is approached as a living organism as if natural forces had shaped the structure.

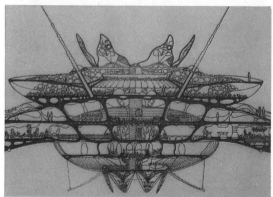

Excavation
The removal of earth from its natural position; the cavity that results from the removal of earth.

Excavation

Exedra
A large niche or recess, either roofed or unroofed, semicircular or rectangular in plan, usually including a bench or seats.

Expansion joint See **Joint**.

Exploded view see **Projection drawing**

Expressionism
A northern European style (1903–1925) that did not treat buildings only as purely functional structures, but as sculptural objects in their own right. Works typical of this style were by Antonio Gaudi in Spain, P.W. Jensen Klint in Denmark, and Eric Mendelsohn and Hans Poelzig in Germany.

Exterior wall See Wall

Extrados
The exterior curve or boundary on the visible face of the arch.

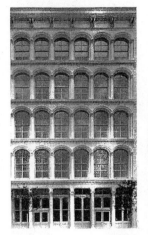

Extradosed arch See Arch.

Eyebrow dormer See Dormer.

Eyebrow window See Window.

F·f

Fabric
An underlying framework or structure consisting of similar connected parts.

Facade
The main exterior face of a building, particularly one of its main sides facing a public way or space, almost always containing one or more entrances and characterized by an elaboration of stylistic details.

Faceted
Shapes that resemble any of the flat, angular surfaces that are similar to those cut on a gemstone.

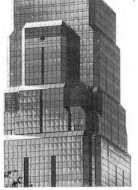

Face brick See Brick.

Face string See String.

Facing
A veneer of nonstructural material forming part of a wall and used as a finishing surface of a rougher or less attractive material, such as stone, terra-cotta, metal, stucco, plaster, and wood.

False arch See Arch.

False attic
An architectural construction concealing a roof, built without windows or enclosing rooms, and located above the main cornice,

False front
A front wall which extends beyond the sidewalls and above the roof of a building to create a more imposing facade.

False window See Window.

Fan tracery See Tracery.

Fanlight
A semicircular window, usually over a door with radiating bars suggesting an open fan.

Fan vault See Vault

Fascia
Any flat horizontal member or molding with minimal projection; any relatively narrow vertical surface which is projected or supported on elements other than a wall below.

Fastener
A mechanical device, weld, bolt, pin or rivet for holding two or more parts, pieces, or members together.

Federal style
Low pitched roofs, a smooth facade and large glass areas characterize this style (1780–1820). Geometric forms accentuate the rhythm of the exterior wall, which is elegant and intentionally austere. Although it rejected Georgian decoration, it retained its symmetry, pilaster-framed entrance, fanlight and sidelights. Windows were simply framed, and quoins were abandoned.

Feline See animal forms.

Fenestra
A loophole in the walls of a fortress or castle, from which missiles were discharged; the ancient equivalent of a window.

Fenestration
The design and placement of windows and other exterior openings in a building.

Fenestration

Ferrous metal   See **Metal.**

Festoon

Hanging clusters of fruit, tied in a bunch with leaves and flowers; used as decoration on pilasters and panels and suspended in a curve between rosettes, skulls of animals, or other decorative elements.

Festoon

Fiberglass   See **Plastic.**

Fieldstone   See **Stone.**

Filigree

Ornamental openwork of delicate or intricate design.

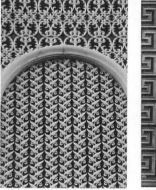

Fillet molding See **Molding**.

Finial
A small, sometimes foliated ornament at the top of a spire, pinnacle or gable which acts as a terminal.

Finish
The texture, color, and other properties of a surface that may affect its appearance.

Fir See **Wood**.

Fireback
The back wall of a fireplace, constructed of heat-resistant masonry or ornamental cast or wrought metal, which radiates heat into the room.

Fire brick See **Brick**.

Fire escape
A continuous, unobstructed path of egress from a building in case of a fire.

Fireplace
An opening at the base of a chimney, usually an open recess in a wall, in which a fire may be built.

Fireplace cheeks
The splayed sides of a fireplace.

Fireproofing
Material applied to structural elements or systems which provides increased fire resistance, usually serving no structural function.

Fire resistance
The capacity of a material or construction to withstand fire or give protection from it; characterized by its ability to confine fire or to continue to perform a structural function.

Fire wall
An interior or exterior wall having sufficiently high fire resistance and structural stability under conditions of fire, to restrict its spread to adjoining areas or adjacent buildings.

Fishscale
An overlapping semicircular pattern in woodwork resembling the scales of fish.

Flagpole
A pole on which a flag, banner or emblem may be raised and displayed; may be self-supporting or attached to a building.

Flamboyant style
The last phase of French Gothic architecture (1450–1500), characterized by flamelike tracery and profuse ornamentation.

Flange
A projecting collar, edge, rib, rim, or ring on a pipe, shaft, or beam.

Flashing
A thin impervious material placed in construction to prevent water penetration or provide water drainage between a roof and walls, and over exterior doors and windows.

Flat arch See **Arch.**

Flat roof See **Roof.**

Fleche
A comparatively small and slender spire, usually located above the ridge of a roof; especially one rising from the intersection of the nave and transcept roofs of Gothic churches.

Flemish bond See **Bond.**

Flemish diagonal bond See **Bond**

Fleur-de-lis ornament See **Ornament.**

Fleuron
The small flower-like shape at the center of each side of the Corinthian abacus.

Flight See **Stair.**

Float glass See **Glass.**

Floor
The lowest surface of a room or structure, as a division between one story and another, made up of a homogeneous material, and usually characterized by a flat surface or a series of flat surfaces at different levels.

Floor

Floor joist See **Joist.**

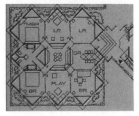

Floor plan
A drawing representing a horizontal section taken above a floor to show, diagrammatically, the enclosing walls of a building, its doors and windows, and the arrangement of its interior spaces.

Floor plan

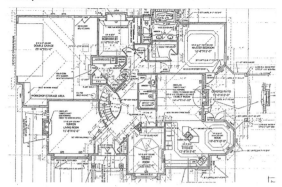

Florentine arch See Arch.

Florentine mosaic See Mosaic.

Floriated
Decorated with floral patterns.

Florid
Highly ornate; extremely rich to the point of overdecoration.

Flue
An incombustible and heat-resistant enclosed passage in a chimney to control and carry away products of combustion from a fireplace to the outside air.

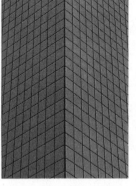

Flush
Signifying that the adjoining surfaces in a building or in a wall are even, level, or arranged so that their edges are close together and on the same plane.

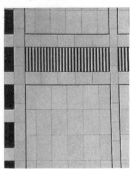

Flush bead molding See Molding.

Flush door See Door.

Flush joint See Joint.

Flush mortar joint See Joint.

Flush paneled door See Door.

Flute
A groove or channel, usually semicircular or semi-elliptical in section; especially one of many such parallel grooves used decoratively, as along the shaft of a column.

Fluting
The hollows or parallel channels cut vertically on the shaft of columns, pilasters and piers, separated by a sharp edge or arris, or by a small fillet.

Flying buttress See Buttress.

Focus
A center of interest or activity drawing attention to the most important aspect of a design scheme, such as the main space, scale, materials, lighting, or orientation.

Foils
In tracery designs, any of several arcs or rounded spaces divided by cusps, tangent to the inner side of a larger arc.

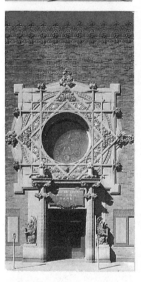

cinquefoil
A five-lobed pattern divided by cusps.

multifoil
Having more than five foils, lobes, or arcuate divisions.

quatrefoil
Having four foils, lobes, or acute divisions.

Folded plate See Wood products.

Folding casement window See Window.

Folding door See Door.

Foliated
Adorned with foils, as on tracery; decorated with a conventionalized representation of leafage, often applied to capitals, friezes, panels, or ornamental moldings.

Folly
A functionally useless, whimsical or extravagant structure, often a fake ruin, sometimes built in a landscaped park to highlight a view, serve as a conversation piece, or commemorate a person or event.

Footing
That portion of the foundation of a structure that transmits loads directly to the soil; may be enlarged to distribute the load over a greater area to prevent or reduce settling.

spread footing
A footing which is especially wide, usually constructed of reinforced concrete.

Forecourt
A court forming an entrance plaza for a single building, or a group of several buildings.

Form
The contour and structure of an object as distinguished from the matter composing it; a distinctive appearance as determined by its visible lines, figure, outline, shape, contour, configuration and profile.

Formal balance See **Balance.**

Formal garden
A garden whose plantings, walks, pools and fountains follow a definite, recognizable plan; frequently symmetrical, emphasizing geometrical forms.

Formalism
A term representing a new classicism in American architecture (1950–1965), manifested in buildings by Mies Van der Rohe, Phillip Johnson, Paul Rudolph and Minuro Yamasaki.

Fort
A fortified place of exclusively military nature.

Fountain

Fortress
A fortification of massive scale, generally of monumental character, and sometimes including an urban core as a protected place of refuge.

Forum
A Roman public square surrounded by monumental buildings, usually including a basilica and a temple; the center of civic life was often purely commercial.

Foundation
The lowest division of a building that serves to transmit and anchor the loads from the superstructure directly to the earth or rock, usually below ground level.

Foundation wall   See Wall.

Fountain
An architectural setting incorporating a continuous or sporadic water supply, fed by a system of pipes and nozzles through which water is forced under pressure to produce a stream of ornamental jets.

Foyer
An entrance way or transitional space from the exterior of a building to the interior spaces.

92

Fractable
A coping on the gable end of a building above the roof, concealing the slope of the roof, and broken into steps or curves forming an ornamental stepped or curving outline.

Frame
The timberwork which encloses and supports structural components of a building.

Framework
Composed of individual parts that are fitted and joined together as skeletal structures designed to produce a specific shape, or to provide temporary or permanent support.

Framing
A system of rough timber structural woodwork that is joined together in order to support or enclose, such as partitions, flooring and roofing. Any framed work, as around an opening in an exterior wall.

Francois I (Premier) style
The culmination of the early phase of French Renaissance architecture (1515–1547), named after Francis I, merged Gothic elements with the full use of Italian decoration. Fontainbleau and the chateaux of the Loire, among them Chambord, are outstanding examples.

Fraternity house
A building used for social and residential purposes by an association of male students called a "fraternity".

Freeform
Shapes that are characterized by a freeflowing rather than a geometric structure, usually resembling forms found in nature.

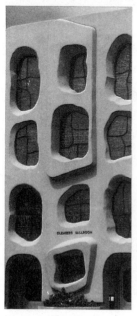

Free-form style
A style (1965–1973) relating to organic and biomorphic forms, such as kidney and boomerang shapes as opposed to rectangular or circular shapes produced by the compass. These forms were also popular in applied arts and the design of furniture.

Freestanding
A structural element which is fixed by its foundation at its lower end, but not otherwise constrained throughout its vertical height.

French arch See Arch.

French door See Door.

Fresco
A mural painted into freshly spread moist lime plaster; in such work ground water-based pigments unite with the plaster base, and retouching is done after it has dried.

Fretting
Decoration produced by cutting away the background of a pattern in stone or wood, leaving the rest as a grating.

Fretwork
A rectangular motif used in early Greek border ornament or pattern, rarely as an isolated ornamental device; an angular counterpart of the spiral or wave.

Frieze
An elevated horizontal continuous band or panel that is usually located below the cornice, and often decorated with sculpture in low relief.

Frontispiece
The decorated front wall or bay of a building; a part or feature of a facade, often treated as a separate element and ornamented highly; an ornamental porch or main pediment.

Frosted
Rusticated, with formalized stalactites or icicles; given an even, granular surface to avoid shine; closely reticulated or matted to avoid transparency.

Functionalism

A design movement (1920–1940) that evolved from several previous movements in Europe, advocating the design of buildings and furnishings as a direct fulfillment of functional requirements, with the construction, materials, and purpose clearly expressed and with aesthetic effect derived chiefly from proportions and finish to the exclusion or subordination of purely decorative effects.

Funk architecture

An alternative form of architecture (1969–1979), using makeshift structures erected from waste materials, was developed by members of rural communes.

Futurist style

A movement (1914–1916) which began with a publication by two young architects, Antonio Sant'Elia and Mario Chiattone, who presented a series of designs for a city of the future. Their manifesto proclaimed that architecture was breaking free from tradition, starting from scratch. It had a preference for what is light and practical. None of these buildings were ever constructed.

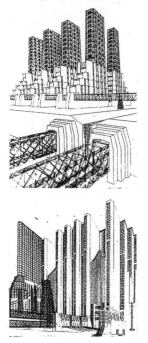

G·g

Gable

The entire triangular end of a wall, above the level of the eaves, the top of which conforms to the slope of the roof which abuts against it, sometimes stepped and sometimes curved in a scroll shape.

dutch gable

A gable, each side of which is multicarved and surmounted by a pediment.

hipped gable

The end of a roof formed into a shape intermediate between a gable and a hip; the gable rises about halfway to the ridge, resulting in a truncated shape, the roof being inclined backward from this level.

Gable roof See **Roof.**

Gabled tower
A tower that is finished with a gable on two or all sides, instead of terminating in a spire.

Gable window See **Window.**

Gaine
A decorative pedestal, taking the place of a column, tapered downward and rectangular in cross section, forming the lower part of a herm, on which a human bust is mounted; often with a capital above.

Gallery
A long covered area acting as a corridor inside or on the exterior of a building or between buildings. A room, often top-lit, used for the display of artwork.

Garage
A building or portion of a residence where motor vehicles are kept; a place for repairing and maintaining vehicles.

Garden
A piece of ground, open or enclosed, appropriated to plants, trees, shrubs, or other landscape features.

Garden apartment
A ground-floor apartment with access to a garden or other adjacent outdoor space; two- or three-story apartment buildings with communal gardens.

Garden house
A summer house in a garden or garden-like situation.

Gargoyle
A spout carrying water from the roofs above, frequently carved with grotesque figures or animals with open mouths, from which water is discharged away from the building's walls.

Garland
An ornament in the form of a bank, wreath, or festoon of leaves, fruits, or flowers.

bay leaf garland
A stylized laurel leaf used in the form of a garland to decorate torus moldings.

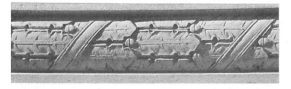

Garret
A room or space located just beneath the roof of a house, usually with sloping ceilings, sometimes called an attic.

Gate
A passageway in a fence, wall, or other barrier which slides, lowers, or swings shut, and is sometime of open construction.

gopuram
In Indian architecture, a monumental gateway tower to a Hindu temple, usually highly decorative.

moon gate
In traditional Chinese architecture a circular opening in a wall.

pai-lou
A monumental Chinese arch or gateway with one, three or five openings erected at the entrance to a palace, tomb, or processional way; usually built of stone in imitation of earlier wood construction.

pai-lou

torana
An elaborately carved ceremonial gateway in Indian Buddhist and Hindu architecture, with two or three lintels between two posts.

tori
A monumental, freestanding gateway to a Shinto shrine, consisting of two pillars with a straight crosspiece at the top and a lintel above it, usually curving upward.

97

Gate house
A building, enclosing or accompanying a gateway for a castle, manor house, or similar building of importance.

Gate tower
A tower containing a gate to a fortress.

Gateway
A passageway through a fence or wall; the structures at an entrance or gate designed for ornament or defense.

Gateway

Gauged brick See **Brick**

Gazebo
A fanciful small structure, used as a summer house, usually octagonal in plan with a steeply pitched roof topped by a finial. The sides are usually open, or latticed between the supports.

Geminated
Coupled, as with columns and capitals.

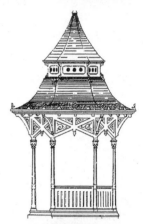

Geminated capital See **Capital.**

Geodesic dome See **Dome.**

Geometric style
The early development of the decorative age of English architecture (1200–1250), characterized by the geometrical forms of its window tracery.

Geometric tracery See **Tracery.**

Geometrical
Refers to forms that can be generated into three-dimensional plane figures, and can be divided into three groups; continuous, such as those used in bands, in enclosed panels, or in flat patterns on walls.

Georgian architecture
A formal arrangement of parts within a symmetrical composition and enriched classical detail characterize this style (1714–1776). The simple facade is often emphasized by a projecting pediment with colossal pilasters and a Palladian window. It often includes dormers, and the entrances are ornately decorated with transoms or fanlights over the doors. The style was transmitted through trade and architectural pattern books.

Gesso
A mixture of gypsum plaster, glue, and whiting; applied as a base coat for decorative painting.

Gibbs surround
The surrounding trim of a doorway or window, consisting of alternating large and small blocks of stone, like quoins; often connected with a narrow raised band along the face of the door, window, or arch.

Gilding
Gold leaf, gold flakes, or brass, applied as a surface finish.

Gingerbread
The highly decorative and often superfluous woodwork applied to a Victorian-style house or commercial structure.

Gingerbread style
A rich and highly decorated style (1830–1880) featuring the ornate woodworking of American buildings, particularly in vogue during the Victorian era.

Girder

A large or principal beam used to support concentrated loads at isolated points along its length.

Girdle

A horizontal band, especially one ringing the shaft of a column.

Girt

In a braced frame, a horizontal member at intermediate level between the columns, studs, or posts; a heavy beam, framed into the studs, which supports the floor joists.

Glass

A hard, brittle, usually transparent or translucent substance, produced by melting a mixture of silica oxides; while molten it may be easily blown, drawn, rolled, pressed, or cast to a variety of shapes. It can be transparent, translucent or mirrored; and made nonglare, pigmented, or tinted. It can be shaped by casting, rolling, pressing or baking. It can also be bonded to metal for use as an exterior cladding.

colored glass

Originated over two thousand years ago when pieces of colored glass were embedded in heavy matrices of stone or plaster.

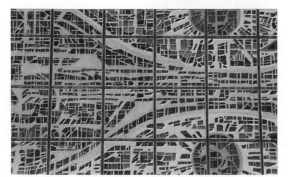

decorative glass

Embossing and sand-blasting techniques create a subtle form of ornamentation. Etching and beveling were also used to create ornamentation in glass.

float glass

A flat glass sheet that is extremely smooth and nearly distortion-free, manufactured by pouring molten glass onto a surface of molten metal and allowing it to cool slowly.

insulating glass

Glass that has insulating qualities, made by sandwiching two layers of glass separated by a vacuum sealed edge.

laminated glass

Two or more plies of flat glass bonded under heat and pressure to interlayers of plastic, to form a shatter-resisting assembly that retains the fragments if the glass is broken; called safety glass.

leaded glass

Dates from the Middle Ages, where glass was set into malleable lead frames.

low-emissivity glass

Glass that transmits visible light while selectively reflecting the longer wavelengths of radiant heat, either by a coating on the glass itself, or on a transparent plastic film in the sealed air space of insulating glass.

obscure glass

Glass that has one or both faces acid-etched or sandblasted to obscure vision.

patterned glass

Glass that has an irregular surface pattern formed in the rolling process to obscure vision or to diffuse light; usually on one side only, the other side is left smooth.

plate glass

A high-quality float glass sheet, formed by rolling molten glass into a plate that is subsequently ground and polished on both sides after cooling.

reflective glass
Window glass having a thin, translucent metallic coating bonded to the exterior or interior surface to reflect a portion of the light and radiant heat and light that strikes it.

sheet glass
A float glass fabricated by drawing the molten glass from a furnace; the surfaces are not perfectly parallel, resulting in some distortion of vision. Used for ordinary window glass.

sound-insulating glass
Glass consisting of two lights in resilient mountings, separated by spacers, and sealed so as to leave an air space between them; the air space contains a dessicant to assure dehydration of the trapped air.

spandrel glass
An opaque glass used in curtain walls to conceal spandrel beams, columns, or other internal structural construction.

stained glass
Glass given a desired color in its molten state, or by firing a stain into the surface of the glass after forming; used in decorative windows or transparent mosaics.

structural glass
Glass which is cast in the form of cubes, rectangular blocks, tile, or large rectangular plates; used widely for wall surfacing.

tempered glass
Annealed glass that is reheated to just below the softening point and then rapidly cooled with water. When fractured, it breaks into relatively harmless pieces.

tinted glass
Glass that has a chemical admixture to absorb a portion of the radiant heat and visible light that strikes it to filter out infrared solar energy, thereby reducing the solar heat gain.

wire glass
Flat or patterned glass having a square or diamond wire mesh embedded within the two faces to prevent shattering in the event of breakage or excessive heat. Wire glass is considered a safety glazing material.

Glass block
Composed of two sheets of plate glass with an air space between them, formed into a sealed modular hollow block; laid up with mortar, similar to masonry blocks as a modular material, and comes in several distinct styles, patterns and degrees of transparency and translucency.

Glass door See **Door**.

Glass mullion system
A glazing system in which sheets of tempered glass are suspended from special clamps, stabilized by perpendicular stiffeners of tempered glass, and joined by a structural silicone sealant or by metal patch plates.

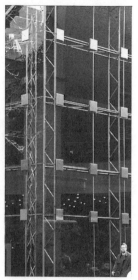

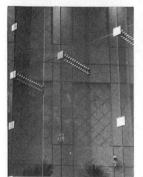

Glaze
A ceramic coating, usually thin, glossy, and glasslike, formed on the surface of pottery earthenware; the material from which the ceramic coating is made.

Glazed brick See **Brick**.

Glazed tile See **Tile**.

Glazed work
Brickwork built with enameled brick or glazed brick.

Glue-laminated arch See **Arch**.

Gneiss See **Stone**.

Gold leaf
Very thin sheets of beaten or rolled gold, used for gilding and inscribing on glass; usually contains a very small percentage of copper and silver. Heavy gold leaf can be classified as gold foil.

Gopuram See **Gate**.

Gorgoneion
In classical decoration the mask of a gorgon, a woman with snakes for hair, believed to avert evil influences.

Gorgoneion

Gothic arch See **Arch**.

Gothic architecture
A revolutionary style of construction of the High Middle Ages in western Europe (1050–1530) which emerged from Romanesque and Byzantine forms. The term "Gothic" was originally applied as one of reproach and contempt. The style was characterized by a delicate balance of thrust and gravity forces. It was most often found in cathedrals employing the rib vault, pointed arches, flying buttresses and the gradual reduction of the walls to a system of richly decorated fenestration. The style's features were height and light, achieved through a mixture of skeletal structures and ever increasing windows. Walls were no longer necessary to support the roof and could be replaced with huge windows of stained glass. One of the finest and oldest French Gothic example is Notre Dame in Paris.

Gothic architecture

Gothic Revival style

Gouache
A method of painting using opaque pigments pulverized in water and mixed with gum.

Granite See **Stone.**

Greek architecture
The first manifestation of this style (800–300 B.C.) was a woode structure of upright posts supporting beams and sloping rafters. The style was later translated into stone elements wit a wood roof. It was a "kit of parts" characterized by austerit and free of ornate carvings. The decorative column orders were an integral part of this style: the Doric, which is the simplest and sturdiest, the Ionic, which was more slender, and the Corinthian, which had a very elaborate capital. Greek ornament is refined in character. The materials were limestone and marble and were prepared with the highest standards of masonry, including sophisticated optical corrections for perspective (entasis).

Gothic Revival style
A romantic style (1830-1860) distinguished by vertically pointed arches, steeply pitched complex gable roofs, finials, and medieval decorative motifs. Country houses featured wide verandas and octagonal towers or turrets.
Windows in dormers had hood molds with gingerbread trim running along the eaves and gable ends. Variety was the standard of the style.

103

Greek architecture

Greek Revival style
The Greek contribution to Neoclassical architecture (1750–1860) stood for a purity and simplicity of structure and form. The buildings are square or rectangular, proportions are broad, details are simple, facades are symmetrical and silhouettes are bold. Free-standing columns support a pedimented gable. Many government and civic buildings are in this style, which is more suited to these building types than to smaller domestic buildings.

Greenhouse
A glass-enclosed, heated structure for growing plants and out-of-season fruits and vegetables under regulated, protected conditions.

Grid
Consists of a framework of parallel, crisscrossed lines or bars forming a pattern of uniform size; sets of intersecting members on a square or triangular matrix, which make up a three-dimensional structural system.

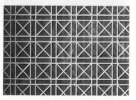

Grid

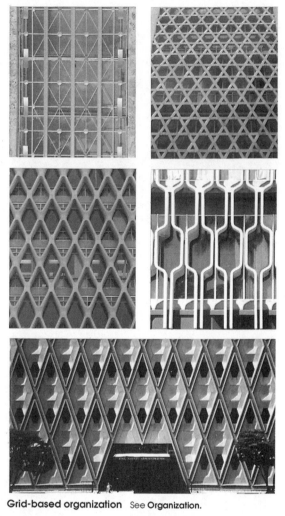

Grid-based organization See **Organization.**

Griffin See **Ornament: animal forms.**

Grille
An ornamental arrangement of bars to form a screen or partition, usually of metal, wood, stone, or concrete, to cover, conceal, decorate, or protect an opening.

Grillwork
Materials arranged with voids to function as, or with the appearance of, a grille.

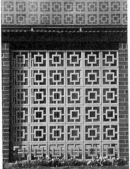

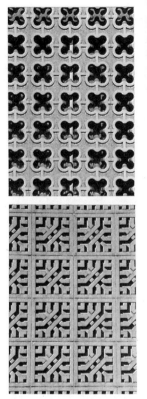

Groin
The curved area formed by the intersection of two vaults.

Groined rib
A rib under the curve of a groin, used as a device to either mask or support it.

Grotesque
Sculptured or painted ornament involving fanciful distortions of human and animal forms sometimes combined with plant motifs, especially those without a counterpart in nature.

Grotto
A natural or artificial cave, often decorated with shells or stones and incorporating waterfalls or fountains.

Groin arch See Arch.

105

Ground joint See Joint.

Ground line see **Perspective projection**

Ground plane see **Perspective projection**

Groundsill
In a framed structure, the sill which is nearest the ground or on the ground; used to distribute the concentrated loads to the foundation.

Grouped columns See **Columns**.

Grouped pilasters See **Pilasters**.

Grout
Mortar containing a considerable amount of water so that it has the consistency of a viscous liquid, permitting it to be poured or pumped into joints, spaces, and cracks within masonry walls and floors.

Grouted masonry
Concrete masonry construction composed of hollow units when the hollow cells are filled with grout.

Guest house
A separate residence for guests, or a small secondary house on a private estate.

Guilloche molding See **Molding**.

Gumwood See **Gumwood**.

Gupta
The dynasty in northern India of the Maurayan empire (320–540), whose court was the center of classical Indian art and literature; the earliest substantial architectural remains are from this period.

Gusset
A plate, usually triangular in shape, used to connect two or more members, or to add strength to a framework at its joints.

Gutta
A small conical-shaped ornament resembling a droplet used in groups under the triglyph or the cornice found in classical architecture.

Gutter
A shallow channel of metal or wood at the edge of a roof eave to catch and drain water into a downspout.

Gymnasium
In Greek and Roman architecture, a large open court for exercise, surrounded by colonnades and rooms for massages and lectures.

Gypsum board
A wallboard having a noncombustible gypsum core, covered on each side with a paper surface.

H·h

Hacienda
A large estate or ranch in areas once under Spanish influence; now the main house on such an estate.

Half column See **Column**.

Half-round molding See **Molding**.

Half-space landing See **Landing**.

Half-timbered
Descriptive of buildings of the 16th and 17th century, which were built with strong timber foundations, supports, knees, and studs, and whose walls were filled in between with plaster or masonry materials.

Half-timbered wall See **Wall**.

Hallway
A corridor or a passageway in a house, hotel, or office, institutional or commercial building.

Hammer brace
A bracket under a hammer beam to support it.

Handrail
A rail providing a handhold and serving as a support at the side of a stair or elevated platform.

Hanger
A strap or rod attached to an overhead structure to support a pipe, conduit, or the framework of a suspended ceiling; a stirrup-like bracket used to support the end of a beam or joist at a masonry wall or girder.

Harmonic proportions
Relates the consonances of the musical harmonic scale to those of architectural design, particularly to theories of proportion.

Harmony
The pleasing interaction or appropriate orderly combination of the elements in a composition.

Haunch
The middle part of an arch, between the springing point and the crown.

Haunch arch   See **Arch**.

Head
In general, the uppermost member of any structure. The upper horizontal cross member between jambs, which forms the top of a door or window frame, may provide structural support for construction above.

Header
A masonry unit laid so that its short end is parallel to the face, overlapping two adjacent widths of masonry; a framing member supporting the ends of joists, transferring the weight of the latter to parallel joists and rafters.

Head mortar joint   See **Mortar joint**.

Hearthstone
A single large stone forming the floor of a fireplace; materials such as firebrick and fireclay products, used to form a hearth.

Heavy-timber construction
Fire-resistant construction obtained by using wood structural members of specified minimum size; wood floors and roofs of specified minimum thickness, and exterior walls of noncombustible construction.

Helix
Any spiral form, particularly a small volute or twist under the abacus of the Corinthian capital.

Hellenic architecture
Architecture (480–323 B.C.) of the classical Greek period up to the death of Alexander the Great.

Hellenistic architecture
The style of Greek architecture (323–30 B.C.) after the death of Alexander the Great.

Hemispherical
A rounded form resembling half of a sphere bounded by a circle.

Hemlock See Wood.

Henry II (Deux) style
The second phase of the early French Renaissance, named after Henry II (1547–1559), who succeded Francis I. It was characterized by Italian classic motifs which supplanted Gothic elements. The west side of the Louvre in Paris is the most characteristic example.

Henry IV (Quatre Style)
The early phase of the classical period of French architecture (1586–1610), preceding the architecture of Louis XIII and Louis LXIV; the style was particularly strong in domestic architecture and town planning.

Herm
A rectangular post, usually of stone, tapering downward, surmounted by a bust of Hermes or other divinity or by a human head.

Herringbone
A way of assembling, in a diagonal zigzag fashion, brick or similar rectangular blocks for paving; also strips of wood or other materials having rectangular shapes for facing walls and ceilings or for use in parquetry.

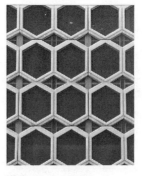

Hickory See Wood.

Hierarchy
An arrangement or system of ranking one above the other or arranged in a graded series or sequence such as size (large to small), shape (similar or dissimilar), and placement (emphasis or location).

Hexagonal
Refers to a plane geometric figure containing six equal sides and six equal angles; occurring in nature as minerals, snow crystals, and honeycombs.

Hieroglyph
A figure representing an idea and intended message; a word or root of a word; a sound which is part of a word, especially applied to the engraved marks and symbols found on the monuments of ancient Egypt.

High Renaissance
Refers to the culmination of the Italian Renaissance style in the late 16th century, characterized by the imitative use of the orders and classical compositional arrangements.

High rise
Describing a building having a comparatively large number of stories, usually above 10–12 stories, and equipped with elevators.

Hinge
A movable joint used to attach, support, and turn a door about a pivot, consisting of two plates joined by a pin which supports the door and connects it to its frame, enabling it to swing open or closed.

Hip
The external angle at the junction of two sloping roofs or sides of a roof; the rafter at the angle where two sloping roofs or sides of a roof meet.

Hip knob   See Ornament.

Hip rafter   See Rafter.

Hip roof   See Roof.

Hipped end
The sloping triangularly shaped end of a hipped roof.

Hipped gable   See Gable.

Hipped gable roof   See Roof.

Hittite architecture
An architecture (2000–1200 B.C.) found in northern Syria and Asia Minor, characterized by fortifications constructed with stone masonry and gateways ornamented with sculpture.

Hollow-core door   See Door.

Hollow molding   See Molding.

Hollow square molding   See Molding.

Hollyhock ornament   See Ornament.

Homestead
A piece of land, limited to 160 acres, deemed adequate for the support of one family.

Homogeneous
Likeness in nature or kind; similar, congruous and uniform in composition or structure throughout.

Honeycomb
Any hexagonal structure or pattern or one resembling such a structure or pattern.

Honeysuckle ornament   See Ornament.

Hood
A projection above an opening, such as a door or window, serving as a screen or as protection against the weather.

Hood mold   See Molding.

Hopper window   See Window.

Horizon line   see Perspective projection

Horizontal cornice   See Cornice.

Horse See **animal forms.**

Horseshoe arch See **Arch.**

Hospital
A building or part thereof used for the medical, obstetrical, or surgical care of patients on a 24 hour basis.

House
A building in which people live.

Hovel
A shed open at the sides and covered overhead for sheltering livestock, produce, or people; a poorly constructed and ill-kept house.

Howe truss See **Truss.**

Human scale See **Scale.**

Hut
A small, simple shelter or dwelling.

Hydraulic elevator
An elevator powered by the energy of a liquid under pressure in a cylinder which acts on a piston or plunger to move the elevator car up and down in guide rails.

Hyperbolic paraboloid
Shapes convoluted in two directions, as opposed to vaulted; having a surface in which all sections parallel to one coordinate plane are hyperbolas, while those parallel to the other plane are parabolas.

Hyperthrum
A latticed window constructed over the door of an ancient building.

Hyperthyrum
A frieze and cornice arranged and decorated in various ways for the lintel of a door.

Hypostyle hall
A structure whose roofing was supported within the perimeter by groups of columns or piers of more than one height; clerestory lights were sometimes introduced; prevalent in ancient Egyptian architecture.

I·i

Igloo
An Eskimo house, constructed of snow blocks or various materials, such as wood, sod, poles and skins; when of snow, a domed structure.

Image See **Design drawing.**

Impost
The horizontal molding or capital on top of a pilaster, pier, or corbel which receives and distributes the thrust at the end of an arch.

Inca architecture
The last of the Pre-Columbian cultures (1200–1400), buildings were characterized by megalithic masonry, as exemplified in the ceremonial buildings of the mountain city Machu Picchu, the last fortress to resist the Spanish invaders.

In cavetto See **Relief**

Incident
Subordinate to the whole scheme, but used to give points of reference along the way, and temporarily create interest.

Indented

A gap left by the omission of stone, brick, or block units in a course of masonry, used for bonding future masonry.

Indented joint See **Joint.**

Indented molding See **Molding.**

Indian (Buddhist) architecture

The earliest surviving buildings (300 B.C.–320 A.D.) are of timber and mud-brick construction, of which the stupa is the most characteristic; it is a hemispherical mound with a processional path around the perimeter and elaborately carved gateways. The most typical is the stupa at Sanchi. In rock-cut Buddhist temples, the main forms and details follow early wooden prototypes, with elaborately carved stone shrines whose exterior is more important than its interior.

Indian (Hindu) architecture

All types of temples in this style (600–1750) consist of a small unlit shrine crowned by a spire and preceded by one or more porchlike halls, used for religious dancing and music. The stone was laid up rough-cut and carved in place by Hindu sculptors who treated every element on every surface as unique, using repetition of sculptural forms to achieve a unifying context. There was no attempt to evolve a style or perfect a particular pillar or column.

Indian (Hindu-Buddhist) architecture

The Hindu and Buddhist religions had a strong influence on Far East temple architecture (1113–1150). One of the most well-known and representative sites is Angkor Wat in Cambodia, a temple complex of shrines intended as a funerary monument. It is perhaps one of the world's largest religious structures and was conceived as a "temple mountain" within an enormous enclosure and surrounded by a wide moat. A monumental causeway formed by giant mythical serpents leads to the entrance gate. The temple is built on a series of stepped terraces, surrounded by towers at each corner. Vaulted galleries receive light from an open colonnade illuminating the continuous relief friezes, which adorn the inner walls. The central sanctuary is a large pagoda-like tower on top of a stepped pyramid. It is joined by passageways to towers at each of four corners at the base.

Indian (Jain) architecture

An architecture (1000–1300) in which temples are enclosed shrines preceded by an open porch, which is often elaborately carved, and have a lighter appearance and are more elegant than Hindu temples.

Indigenous American architecture

The native styles (500 B.C.–1500 A.D.) range from the wigwams and longhouses of forested areas, teepees of the Plains Indians, igloos of the Eskimos; and the sophisticated communal pueblo cities carved out of mountainsides or built out of adobe in the Southwest.

Indus Valley architecture

Cities that flourished in the Indus Valley (1500–1200 B.C.) were carefully planned on a grid system, with main boulevards forming rectangular blocks; they were mostly of mud-brick construction.

Industrial Revolution style

The evolution of this style (1750–1890) was based on the production of iron and steel in quantities that could be used as a primary building material. The first iron frame structures were industrial buildings, which evolved into the steel frame skyscrapers of modern times. The few pioneers of this new style were engineers and not architects. Walls were still made of masonry over a steel skeleton, and the use of large glass skylights was widespread.

Industrial design

Utilizing the resources of technology to create and improve products and systems which serve humans, taking into account factors such as safety, economy, and efficiency in production, distribution, and use.

Informal balance   See **Balance.**

Inlay

A shaped piece of one material embedded in another, usually in the same plane, as part of a surface ornamentation.

Inn
A place which provides eating and drinking, but no lodging, for the public; a tavern.

Inscription
Lettering that is carved or engraved in stone, wood, or on the surface of other materials, often of monumental scale, used primarily on exterior surfaces.

Insulated column   See **column**

Insulating glass   See **Glass.**

Intaglio
Incised carving in which the forms are hollowed out of the surface; the relief in reverse, often used as a mold.

Integrated ceiling
A suspended ceiling system in which acoustical, illumination, and air-handling components are combined as an integral part of a grid.

Intercolumniation
The clear distance between two columns, measured at the lower part of the shafts, according to a system of proportions in classical architecture, based on the diameter of the column as the governing module.

Interdome   See **Dome.**

Interfenestration
The space between the windows and their decorations on a facade.

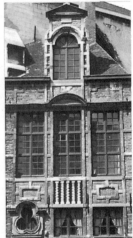

Interior door   See **Door.**

Interior wall   See **Wall.**

Interlace
An ornament of bands or stalks elaborately intertwined, sometimes including fantastic images.

113

Interlaced

Intermixed forms that cross over each other with alternation as if woven together.

Interlaced arches

Arches, usually circular, pointed, or foliated, so constructed on their supports that their forms intersect each other.

Interlaced ornament

A band of ornamental figures that are overlapped or intertwined to create resultant forms.

Interlocked

Two or more components, members, or items of equipment which are arranged mechanically or electrically to operate in some specific relationship with each other.

Interlocking

Forms that are united firmly or joined closely by hooking or dovetailing.

Interlocking joint See **Joint**.

International style

A style of architecture (1920–1945) in Europe and America pioneered by Le Corbusier, which spread to the Bauhaus, where it was most influential. It was characterized by an emphasis on function and a rejection of traditional decorative motifs and regional characteristics. It was further characterized by flat roofs, smooth and uniform surfaces, large expanses of windows and projecting or cantilevered upper floors. The complete absence of ornamentation is typical, and cubistic shapes were fashionable. White was the preferred color. Horizontally emphasized windows turning around corners were favored. Roofs without eaves terminate flush with the plane of the wall. Wood and metal casement windows were set flush to the wall as well. Sliding windows were popular, and clerestory windows were also used. There were fixed panes of glass from floor to ceiling, and curtain-like walls of glass were common. Popular building materials were reinforced concrete, steel frames, and an unprecedented use of pre-fabricated parts, since the style had its roots in industrial architecture. The resultant forms were much akin to cubist and abstract art.

International style

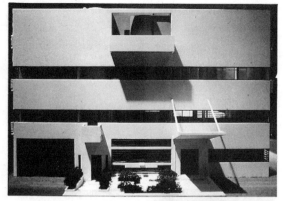

Interrupted arch
A segmental pediment whose center has been omitted, often to accommodate an ornament.

Intersecting tracery See **Tracery.**

Interstitial
Forming a narrow or small space between parts or other elements, or between floors in a structure.

Interweaving counterpoint See **Counterpoint.**

Intonaco See **Plaster.**

Intrados
The inner curve or face of an arch or vault forming the concave underside.

Inverted arch See **Arch.**

Invisible architecture
A form of architecture that would represent an expenditure of energy to create walls and furniture by the use of jets of air instead of conventional building materials, and allow for instant buildings.

Ionic order
An order of architecture invented by the Greeks, distinguished by an elegantly molded base; tall, slender shafts with flutes separated by fillets; and capitals, using a spiral volute which supports an architrave with three fascias; an ornamental frieze, and a cornice corbeled out on egg-and-dart and dentil moldings.

115

Ionic order

Iranian architecture
Decorative patterned brickwork, colored tile and molded stucco characterize this style (500–1000). Other attributes are the use of stalactite vaults. The essential elements are richly decorated surfaces, brightly colored tiles and molded stucco. The minaret evolved into a standard form that had an influence on Indian architecture.

Iron   See **Metal**.

Iron Age
The period (700 B.C.) characterized by the introduction of iron metallurgy for tools and weapons.

Ironwork
Wrought iron or cast iron, usually decorative, often elaborate.

Islamic architecture
Mesopotamian and Graeco-Roman forms are the two main sources for this style (600–1500), which makes use of symbolic geometry, using pure forms such as the circle and square. The major sources of decorative design are floral motifs, geometric shapes and Arabic calligraphy. The major building types are the mosque and the palace. Mosque plans are based on strongly symmetrical layouts featuring a rectangular courtyard with a prayer hall. Forms are repetitive and geometrical; the surfaces are richly decorated with glazed tiles, carved stucco and patterned brickwork, or bands of colored stonework. Plaster made from gypsum was carved and highly polished to give it a marblelike finish.

Isolation joint See **Joint.**

Isometric projection see **Projection drawing**

Italianate style
A style (1840–1880) typified by a rectangular two- or three-story house with wide eaves supported by large brackets, tall, thin first-floor windows, and a low pitched roof topped with a cupola. There are pronounced moldings, details and rusticated quoins. Earmarks of the style are arched windows with decorative "eyebrows" and recessed entryways. The style appeared in cast-iron facades, whose mass produced sections featured stylized classical ornament.

Italian Villa style
The main feature of this style (1830–1880) is the combination of a tall tower with a two-story "L"- or "T"- shaped floor plan. Gently pitched roofs resembling the pediment of classical temples had wide projecting eaves. Windows are grouped into threes or placed within arcades. A smooth stucco finish highlighted classic simplicity, while exuberant ornamentation recalls the baroque. The overall massing is asymmetrical, intending to produce a picturesque quality.

J·j

Jack rafter See **Rafter.**

Jacobean style
An English architectural and decorative style (1600–1625) adapting the Elizabethan style to continental Renaissance influence, named after James I.

Jamb
The vertical member at the side of a window, door, chimney, or other exterior opening.

Jamb shaft
A small shaft having a capital and a base, placed against the jamb of a door or window.

Japanese architecture
An architecture (500–1700) based exclusively on timber construction, strongly influenced by Chinese design. Simple pavilion structures consist of a wooden framework of uprights and tie beams supported by a wooden platform. Nonbearing walls are constructed of plaster and wood, and sliding partitions of light translucent screens divide interior spaces, with doors and windows of lightweight material. Tiled hipped roofs project wide overhangs with upturned eaves as the result of elaborate bracket systems. Stone is used only for bases, platforms, and fortification walls. Great emphasis is placed on the integration of buildings with their surroundings, with open verandas providing the transition. There is a strictly modular approach to the layout, based on the tatami mat, which governs the entire design of the house. Carpenters became skilled in designing individual types of wooden joints.

Japanese architecture

Joggle joint See **Joint.**

Joggle post
A post made of two or more pieces joggled together.

Jogglework
A stone keyed by joggles.

Joint
The space between the stones in masonry, or bricks in brickwork. In concrete work, joints control the shrinkage on large areas, and isolate independent elements.

angle joint
Any joint formed by uniting two members at a corner which results in a change of direction.

blind joint
A joint that is invisible.

butt joint
A plain square joint between two members, when the contact surfaces are cut at right angles to the faces of the pieces; the two are filled squarely against each other rather than lapped.

cogged joint
A carpentry joint formed by two crossed structural members, each of which is notched at the place where they cross.

construction joint
A separation provided in a building which allows its component parts to move with respect to each other; a joint where two placements of concrete meet.

control joint
A joints that is pre-molded, tooled, or sawed, and installed to prevent shrinkage of large areas. It creates a deliberately weakened section to induce cracking at the chosen location rather than at random.

dovetail joint
A splayed tenon, shaped like a dove's tail, broader at its end than at its base; the joint is formed by such a tenon fitting into the recess of a corresponding mortise.

expansion joint
A joint designed to permit the expansion or contraction due to temperature changes. It generally extends through the entire structure from the footings to the roof.

flush joint
Any joint finished even or level with the surrounding surfaces.

indented joints
A joint used in joining timbers end to end; a notched fishplate is attached to one side of the joint to fit into two corresponding notches in the joined timbers, the entire assembly is fastened with bolts.

interlocking joint
A form of joggle in which a protrusion on one member complements a slot or routed groove in another; a joint formed between sheet-metal parts by joining their preformed edges to provide a continuous locked piece.

isolation joint
A joint that separates one concrete section from another so that each one can move independently; found in floors, at columns, and at junctions between the floor and walls.

joggle joint
A notch or projection in one piece of material which is fitted to a projection or notch in a second piece, to prevent one piece from slipping past the other.

lap joint
A joint in which one member overlaps the edge of another and is connected.

miter joint
A joint between two members at an angle to each other; each member is cut at an angle equal to half the angle of the junction; usually at right angles to each other.

mortise and tenon
A joint between two members, formed by fitting a tenon at the end of one member into a mortise cut into the other.

spline joint
A joint formed by inserting a spline of long strips of wood or metal in a slot cut into the two butting members.

standing seam joint
In metal roofing, a type of joint between the adjacent sheets of material, made by turning up the edges of two adjacent sheets and then folding them over.

tongue and groove joint
A joint formed by the insertion of the tongue of one member into the corresponding groove of another.

Jointing
In masonry, the finishing of joints between courses of bricks or stones before the mortar has hardened.

Joist
One of a series of parallel timber beams used to support floor and ceiling loads, and supported in turn by larger beams, girders, or bearing walls; the widest dimension is placed in the vertical plane.

ceiling joist
Any joist which carries a ceiling; one of several small beams to which the ceiling of a room is attached. They are mortised into the sides of the main beams or suspended from them by strap hangers.

floor joist
Any joist or series of joists which supports a floor.

trimming joist
A joist supporting one end of a header at the edge of an opening in a floor or roof frame, parallel to the other common joists.

Juxtaposition
The state or position of being placed close together or side by side, so as to permit comparison or contrast.

K·k

Key console
A console which acts as the keystone of an arch.

Key course
A continuous course of keystones in an arch, used in a deep archway where a single keystone will not suffice; a course of keystones used in the crown of a barrel vault.

Keystone
The central stone or voussoir at the top of the arch, the last part to be put into position to lock the arch in place, often embellished with a human face.

Kinetic architecture
A style (1971–1985) depicted by forms which are dynamic, adaptable and responsive to the changing demands of the users. The broad category includes a number of other concepts, such as mobile architecture, which would not necessarily be constantly moving, only capable of being moved if required.

King closure   See **Brick**.

Kiosk
A small ornamented pavilion or gazebo, usually open for the sale of merchandise, or to provide cover or shelter to travelers.

Knee brace   See **Brace**.

Kneestone
A stone which is sloped on top and flat on the bottom that supports inclined coping on the side of a gable, or a stone that breaks the horizontal joint pattern to begin the curve of an arch.

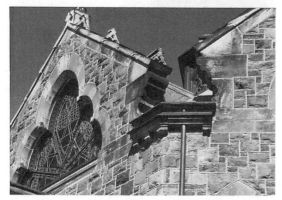

Knob
A protuberance, useful or ornamental, which forms the termination of an isolated member; a handle, more or less spherical, used for operating the mechanism for opening a door.

Knot ornament   See **Ornament**.

Knotwork
A carved ornamental arrangement of cordlike figures joined together to form a type of fringe, used to decorate voussoirs and moldings.

Kumimono
In traditional Japanese construction, a system of supports composed of weight-bearing blocks and bracket arms.

L·l

Label molding   See Molding.

Label stop
The termination of a hood-mold or arched dripstone in which the lower ends are turned in a horizontal direction away from the door or window opening.

Labyrinth
A maze of twisting passageways; a garden feature of convoluted paths outlined by hedges, often with a garden house at the center; in medieval cathedrals, the representation of a maze inlaid in the floor.

Lacework
Architectural patterns or decorations resembling lace.

Lacing course
A course of brick or tile inserted in a rough stone or rubble course as a bond course.

Lally column   See Column.

Lambs tongue
The end of a handrail which is turned out or down from the rail and curved to resemble a tongue.

Laminated glass   See Glass

Lanai
A living room or lounge area which is entirely, or in part, open to the outdoors.

Lancet arch   See Arch.

Lancet window   See Window.

Landing
The horizontal platform at the end of a stair flight or between two flights of stairs.

half-space landing
A stair landing at the junction of two flights which reverses direction, making a turn of 180 degrees. Such a landing includes the width of both flights, plus the well.

quarter-space landing
A square landing connecting two flights of stairs that continue in a straight line.

Landmark
Any building structure or place which has a special character or special historic or aesthetic interest or value as part of the heritage or cultural characteristics of a city, state, or nation.

Landscape architect
A person trained and experienced in the design and development of landscape and gardens; a designation reserved for a person professionally licensed to perform landscape architectural services.

Lantern
A tower or small turret with windows or openings for light and air, crowning a dome or cupola.

Lap joint See Joint.

Lap splice See Splice.

Larch See Wood

Lateral brace See Brace.

Latin cross
A cross which has an upright much longer than the cross-beam; three arms are the same length, and the fourth lower arm is much longer.

Lattice
A network of bars, straps, rods, or laths crossing over and under one another; the result is a rectangular or diagonal checkered pattern, which may be varied by the width of the bands and the spacing of the members.

Lattice dome See Dome.

Lattice molding See Molding.

Lattice truss See Truss.

Latticed window See Window.

Latticework
Reticulated or netlike work formed by the crossing of laths or thin strips of wood or iron, usually in a diagonal pattern.

Lead See Metal.

Leaded glass See Glass.

Leaded light
A window having small diamond-shaped or rectangular panes of glass set in lead canes.

Lean-to
A shed or building having a single pitched roof, with its highest end against an adjoining wall or building.

Lean-to roof See Roof.

Lesche
In ancient Greece, a public portico or clubhouse, frequented by people for conversation or hearing the news; such buildings were numerous in cities, and their walls were decorated by celebrated painters.

Lift-slab construction
Casting floor and roof slabs one upon another, then jacking or hoisting them into final position, saving on formwork for cast-in-place floors in a multistory structure.

Light
An opening through which daylight is admitted to the interior space of a building; a pane of glass, window, or compartment of a window.

Light fixture
A luminaire secured in place or attached as a permanent appendage or appliance. It consists of a lighting unit with lamps and components to protect the electrical circuits from the weather, and other devices to spread the light in a prescribed pattern.

Light fixture

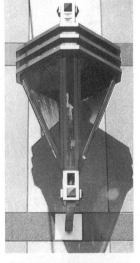

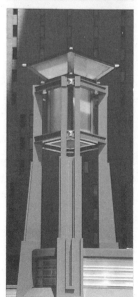

Limba   See **Wood.**

Limestone   See **Stone.**

Line
The path of a point extended through space; it may be geometric (straight lines and arcs), free form (flowing and curving), or a combination of the two.

Lineal organization   See **Organization.**

Linear
Forms that describe a line, are related to a line, or are defined by being arranged in a line.

Lining
Material which covers any interior surface, such as a framework around a door or window or boarding that covers interior surfaces of a building.

Linked organization   See **Organization.**

Lintel
The horizontal beam that forms the upper structural member of an opening for a window or door and supports part of the structure above it.

Lintel course
In stone masonry, a course set at the level of a lintel, commonly differentiated from the wall by its greater projection, its finish, or thickness, which often matches that of the lintel.

Load-bearing wall   See **Wall.**

Lobby
A space at the entrance to a building, theater, hotel, or other structure.

Lock
A device which fastens a door, gate, or window in position; may be opened or closed by a key or a dead bolt.

Locust See Wood.

Loft
An open space beneath a roof, often used for storage; one of the upper floors of a warehouse or factory, typically unobstructed except for columns, with high ceilings; the upper space in a church, choir or organ loft.

Log house
A house built of logs which are horizontally laid and notched and fitted at the ends to provide stability.

Loggia
An arcaded or colonnaded structure, open on one or more sides, sometimes with an upper story; an arcaded or colonnaded porch or gallery attached to a larger structure.

Lombard architecture
A north Italian pre-Romanesque architecture (600–700) during the rule of the Lombards, based on early Christian and Roman forms, and characterized by the development of the ribbed vault and the vaulting column shaft.

Longhouse
A communal dwelling characteristic of many early cultures, consisting of a wooden, bark-covered framework often as much as 100 feet in length.

Longitudinal section see Projection drawing

Loop window See Window.

Loophole
Any opening in a parapet or wall to allow for vision, light or air.

Lotus capital See Capital.

Louis XIV-XVI style
A high classical style (1643–1792) typified in the architecture, decoration and furniture of France, culminating in the building of Versailles. It developed into the Rococo style.

Louver
A window opening made up of overlapping boards, blades or slats, either fixed or adjustable, designed to allow ventilation in varying degrees without letting in the rain.

Louvered door See Door.

Low-emissivity glass See Glass.

Lozenge
An equilateral four-sided figure with pairs of equal angles, two acute and two obtuse; a rhombic or diamond-shaped figure.

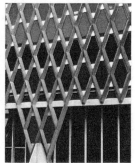

Lucarne window See **Window.**

Lucite See **Plastic.**

Lumber
Timber sawn or split in the form of beams, boards, joists, planks, or shingles; refers especially to pieces smaller than heavy timber.

Lunette
A crescent or semicircular window or wall panel framed by an arch or vault.

M·m

Machicolation
Openings formed by setting the parapets out on corbels so as to project beyond the face of the wall; parapets set out on corbels have a similar appearance, even if there are no openings.

Machu Picchu
The most celebrated Inca citadel, on a promontory 2,000 feet above the valley in the Andes in Peru. The site includes buildings which surround an oblong plaza. The houses were built around courts, with stairs, windows, interior niches, narrow doorways, and thatch-covered gable roofs. Some houses were carved out of the rock, some connecting stairs are hewn out of the mountain.

Mahogany See **Wood.**

Maltese cross
A cross formed by four equal triangles or arrowheads joined at their points; the outer edge of each arm is indented with an angle.

Manastaba
In Indian architecture, a free-standing pillar in front of a temple.

Mandapa
In Indian architecture, a large porchlike hall leading to a Hindu temple and used for religious dancing and music.

Mannerism
A style of Italian architecture (1530–1600) which was a reaction against the classical perfection of High Renaissance architecture, either responding with a rigorous application of classical rules and motifs or flaunting classical convention in terms of shape and scale. It was a relaxed nonconformist style, using unnatural proportion and willful stylistic contradictions.

Mannerism

Manor house
The house occupied by the lord of a manor; the most important house in a country or village neighborhood.

Mansard roof See **Roof.**

Mansion
A large and imposing dwelling; a large apartment in a building.

Mantel
The beam or arch which serves as a support for the masonry above a fireplace; a mantelpiece.

Mantelpiece
The fittings and decorative elements of a mantel, including the cornice and shelf carried above the fireplace.

Manueline architecture
The last phase (1495–1521) of Gothic architecture in Portugal, so named after King Manuel.

Maple See **Wood.**

Marble See **Stone**

Margin draft
A narrow dressed border along the edge of a squared stone, usually the width of a chisel, as a border surrounding the rough central portion.

Marmoset
An antic figure, usually grotesque, introduced into architectural decoration in the 13th century.

Marquee
A permanent projecting rooflike shelter over an entrance to a building, often displaying information about performances.

Marquetry
Inlaid pieces of a material, such as wood or ivory, fitted together and glued to a common background.

Mascaron
The representation of a face, a human or partly human head, more or less caricatured, and used as an architectural element.

Mask
A corbel, the shadow of which bears a close resemblance to that of a human face. It was a favorite ornament under the parapet of a chancel.

Masonite See Wood products.

Masonry
Includes all stone products, all brick products and all concrete block units, including decorative and customized blocks.

ashlar masonry
Smooth square stones laid with mortar in horizontal courses.

broken rangework masonry
Stone masonry laid in horizontal courses of different heights, any one course of which may be broken into two or more courses.

cavity wall masonry
An exterior wall of masonry, consisting of an outer and inner course separated by a continuous air space, connected together by wire or sheet-metal ties; the dead air space provides improved thermal insulation.

concrete masonry
Construction consisting of concrete masonry units laid up in mortar or grout.

coursed masonry
Masonry construction in which the stones are laid in regular courses, not irregularly as in rough or random stonework.

coursed rubble masonry
Masonry construction in which roughly dressed stones of random size are used, as they occur, to build up courses; the interstices between them are filled with smaller pieces or with mortar.

cyclopean masonry
Often found in ancient cultures, characterized by huge irregular stones laid without mortar and without any form of coursing.

diamondwork masonry
Masonry construction in which pieces are set to form diamond-shaped patterns on the face of the wall.

pebble wall masonry
A wall built of pebbles set in mortar, or one faced with pebbles embedded in a mortar coating on the exposed surface, either at random or in a pattern.

pitch-faced masonry
In masonry, a surface in which all arrises are cut true and in the same plane, but the face beyond the arris edges is left comparatively rough, dressed with a chisel.

polygonal masonry
Masonry constructed of stones having smooth polygonal surfaces.

quarry-faced masonry
Squared blocks with rough surfaces that look as if they just came out of the ground.

random ashlar masonry
Ashlar masonry in which regular stones are set without continuous joints and appear to be laid without a drawn pattern, although the pattern may be repeated.

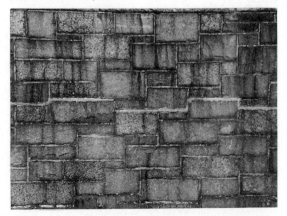

rubble masonry
Very irregular stones, used primarily in the construction of foundations and walls where the irregular quality is desirable.

rubblework
Stone masonry built entirely of rubble.

rusticated masonry
Coursed stone in which each block is separated by deep joints. The surface is usually very rough.

rustic stone masonry
Any rough, broken stone suitable for rustic masonry, most commonly limestone or sandstone; usually set with the longest dimension exposed horizontally.

square rubble masonry
Wall construction in which squared stones of various sizes are combined in patterns that make up courses at every third or fourth stone.

vermiculated masonry
A form of masonry surface, incised with wandering, discontinuous grooves resembling worm tracks; a type of ornamental winding frets or knots on mosaic pavements, resembling the tracks of worms.

Masonry Field
In brickwork, the expanse of wall between openings, principally composed of stretchers.

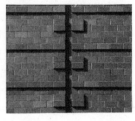

Masonry wall See Wall

Mass
The physical volume or bulk of a solid body, or a grouping of individual parts or elements that compose a body of unspecified size.

Mastaba
A freestanding tomb found in ancient Egypt, consisting of a rectangular superstructure with inclined sides, from which a shaft leads to underground burial chambers.

Mastic
Any heavy-bodied, dough-like adhesive compound; a sealant with putty-like properties used for applying tiles to a surface, or for weatherproofing joints.

Mausoleum
A large and stately tomb, or a building housing such a tomb, or tombs; originally the tomb for King Mausolos of Caria, about 350 B.C.

Mayan arch See Arch.

Mayan architecture
Sites such as Tikal in Guatemala, Copan in Honduras, and Palenque represent the highest development of this style (600–900). It is characterized by monumental constructions including soaring temple pyramids, palaces with sculptural facades, ritual ball courts, plazas and interconnecting quadrangles. Buildings were erected on platforms, often with a roof structure. The lower section contained a continuous frieze carrying intricate decoration of masks, human figures, and geometric forms. Decorative elements formed open parapets. Exterior surfaces were covered with a lime stucco and painted in bright colors, and interior walls were massive and decorated. The sites were totally rebuilt periodically, leaving previous structures completely covered and intact. One of the most notable examples is Chichen Itza in Yucatan, the largest center of the Mayan civilization.

Mayan architecture

Maze
A confusing and intricate plan of hedges in a garden, usually above eye level, forming a labyrinth.

Meander
A running ornament consisting of a fret design with many involved turnings and an intricate variety of designs.

Measuring line see **Perspective projection**

Medallion
An ornamental plaque, usually round or oval in shape, inscribed with an object in low relief, such as a head, flower or figure, and applied to a wall or frieze.

Medallion

Medallion molding See **Molding.**

Medieval architecture
The architecture of the European Middle Ages (400–1400); the use of Byzantine, Romanesque and Gothic elements spanned a millennium. It was an age of the fortified castle, where bishop's palaces rivalled cathedrals in splendor and served public and private functions. As population grew, smaller houses nestled around castle walls, creating medieval towns. As urban land grew more valuable, tall narrow houses with upper stories were common.

Medusa
In Greek mythology, the mortal one of the three Gorgons, who had snakes for hair and whose head was cut off by Perseus to present to Athena as an ornament for her shield.

Meeting house
A house of worship, especially that of the Society of Friends or Quakers and the Mormons.

Megalithic
Built of unusually large stones, used as found in nature or roughly hewn, especially as used in ancient construction.

Megastructure
A type of structure (1964–1976) in which individual buildings become merely components or lose their individuality altogether. Vast new structures were proposed to replace existing cities. Their overall purpose is to provide a total environment for work and leisure.

Megastructure

Membrane
A thin, flexible surface such as a net or form with a fabric surface, supported by tension cables or by an air system.

Memorial
An architectural or sculptural object or plaque commemorating a person or an event.

Memorial arch
An arch commemorating a person or event, popular during the Roman Empire and again at the time of Napoleon.

Merlon
In an embattled parapet, one of the solid alternates between two crenels, or open spaces.

Meshrebeeyeh
In Islamic countries, an elaborately turned or carved wood screen or wood lattice which encloses a balcony window.

Mesoamerican architecture
A characteristic feature of this architecture (1300–500 B.C.) is the great temple pyramids of Pre-Columbian America, which are equivalent in complexity to those of ancient Egypt and the Middle East. The main centers in Mexico and Peru are divided into four main cultures: Mayan, Toltec, Aztec, and Inca. All four civilizations conceived of their architecture in monumental terms characterized by strong grid plans, huge walled enclosures, and vast stone cities.

Mesolithic Era
The cultural period between the Paleolithic and Neolithic eras, marked by the appearance of cutting tools.

Mesopotamian architecture
A massive architecture (3000–500 B.C.) constructed of mud-bricks set with clay mortar, producing heavy walls articulated by pilasters and recesses and faced with glazed brick. Columns were seldom used, and openings were infrequent and small.

Metal-clad door See **Door.**

Metals
Any of a class of elementary substances which are crystalline when solid and characterized by opacity, ductility and conductivity; mined in a form called "ore" and manufactured to specific applications.

aluminum
A lightweight metal, used in minor structural framing, curtain walls, window frames, doors, flashing and many types of hardware.

brass
Any copper alloy having zinc as the principal alloying element, but often with small quantities of other elements.

bronze
An alloy of copper and tin, bronze in color, having a substantial admixture of copper to modify the properties of the principal element, as aluminum bronze and magnesium bronze.

cast iron
A hard, nonmalleable iron alloy containing carbon and silicon, which is poured into a sand mold and then machined to a desired architectural shape.

copper
A metal with good electrical conductivity, used for roofing, flashing, hardware and plumbing applications; when exposed to air, copper oxidizes and develops a greenish "patina" that halts corrosion.

ferrous metal
Metal in which iron is the principal element.

iron
A metalic element found in the earth's crust, consisting of a malleable, ductile, magnetic substance from which pig iron and steel are manufactured.

lead
A soft, malleable, heavy metal; has a low melting point and a high coefficient of thermal expansion; very easy to cut and work.

stainless steel
A high-strength, tough steel alloy; contains chromium with nickel as an additional alloying element; highly resistant to corrosion and rust.

steel
A hard and malleable metal when heated, produced by melting and refining according to the carbon content; used for structural shapes due to its high tensile strength malleable alloy of iron and carbon.

tin
A lustrous white, soft, and malleable metal having a low melting point; relatively unaffected by exposure to air; used for making alloys and solder, and in coating sheet metal.

weathering steel
A high-strength, low-alloy steel that forms an oxide coating when exposed to rain or moisture in the atmosphere, which adheres to the base metal and protects it from further corrosion.

wrought iron
A commercially pure iron of fibrous nature, valued for its corrosion resistance and ductility; used for water pipes, water tank plates, rivets, and forged work.

zinc
A hard bluish-white metal, brittle at normal temperatures, very malleable and ductile when heated; not subject to corrosion; used for galvanizing sheet steel and iron, in various metal alloys.

Metope
A panel, either plain or decorated with carvings, between triglyphs in Doric frieze.

Mews
An alley or court in which stables are or once were located or have been converted into residences.

133

Mezzanine
A low-ceilinged story located between two main stories, usually constructed directly above the ground floor, often projecting over it as a balcony.

Mezzo-relievo See **Relief.**

Mihrab
A niche in the mosque of any religious Muslim building, indicating the direction of prayer toward Mecca.

Milling
In stonework, the processing of quarry blocks, through sawing, planing, turning, and cutting techniques, to produce finished stone.

Minaret
The tall slender tower of a mosque with stairs leading up to one or more balconies from which followers are called to prayer.

Minoan architecture
A Bronze Age civilization (1800–1300 B.C.) which flourished in Crete, whose gate buildings with porches provided access to unfortified compounds. Foundation walls, piers and lintels were stone with upper walls framed in timber. Rubble masonry was faced with stucco and decorated with wall frescoes. Ceilings were wood, as were the many columns with balloon capitals, and featuring a distinct downward tapering shaft, as in the Palace of King Minos at Knossos.

Mission
A diplomatic office in a foreign country; a small church or monastic order.

Mission architecture
The church and monastery architecture of the Spanish religious orders in Mexico and California in the 18th century.

Mission style
A characteristic of this style (1890–1920) is its simplicity of form. Round arches supported by piers form openings in the thick stucco walls, with roof eaves extending beyond the wall surface. Towers, curvilinear gables and small balconies were used on large buildings. The only ornamentation is a plain string course that outlines arches or gables or balconies.

Mission tile See **Tile**

Miter
The line formed by the meeting of moldings or other surfaces which intersect each other at an angle; each member is cut at exactly half the angle of the junction.

Mixtec architecture
An architecture (700–1000) characterized by great mass, use of interior stone columns, and emphasis on horizontal lines was developed in Oaxaca, Mexico. The minutely detailed fretwork of the interior and exterior paneled friezes was produced by assembling thousands of small decorative elements and setting them into clay. At Mitla there are freestanding buildings surrounding large courts oriented towards the cardinal points of the compass.

Moat
A broad, deep trench, filled with water, surrounding the ramparts of a town or fortress.

Mock-up See **Design drawing.**

Model See **Design drawing.**

Modernism
A term meaning "just now." The Modern Movement (1960–1975) was the conscious attempt to find an architecture tailored to modern life and one that made use of new materials. It rejected the concept of applied style and the use of ornament. It used concrete, steel and glass to help evolve an architecture more directly related to construction methods. Exterior, interior and forms were conceived and expressed as a single entity.

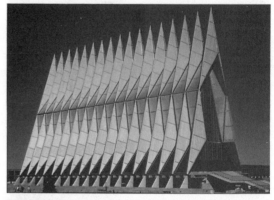

Modernistic style

A style (1920–1940) characterized by a mode of ornamentation combining rectilinear patterns and zigzags with geometrical curves. One of the distinctive forms consisted of polychrome low-relief frames. Ornamentation around doors and windows and on panels stresses the verticality in skyscraper designs. Stepped setbacks are also common, reflecting local urban zoning ordinances.

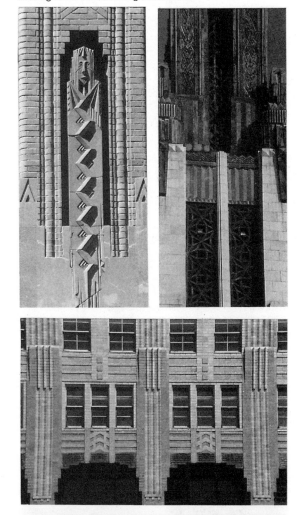

Modillion

A horizontal bracket or console, usually in the form of a scroll with acanthus, supporting the corona under a cornice.

Modular brick   See **Brick.**

Modular system

A method of designing or constructing buildings and equipment in which standardized modules are widely used.

Modulation

To measure, to adjust to, or regulate by a certain proportion; to temper or to soften in passing from one element, form, or material to another.

Module

A simple ratio by which all interchangeable parts of a building are related as part of an ordered system.

Modulor

A system of proportion developed by Le Corbusier in 1942. It was based on the theories of early civilizations and on the human form, and was related to the golden section.

Mogul architecture

The later phase of Indian Islamic architecture, named after the Mogul dynasty, typified by monumental palaces and mosques and detailed decorative work. The Taj Mahal is the most famous example.

Molded brick See **Brick.**

Molding
A decorative profile given to architectural members and subordinate parts of buildings, whether cavities or projections, such as cornices, bases, or door and window jambs and heads.

backband molding
A piece of millwork used around a rectangular window or door casing to cover the gap between the casing and the wall, or as a decorative feature.

band molding
A small broad, flat molding, projecting slightly, of rectangular or slightly convex profile, used to decorate a surface, either as a continuous strip or formed into various shapes.

bar molding
A rabbeted molding applied to the edge of a bar or counter to serve as a nosing.

base molding
Molding used to trim the upper edge of an interior baseboard.

bead molding
A narrow wood drip molded on one edge, against which a door or window closes; a stop bead; a strip of metal or wood used around the periphery of a pane of glass to secure it in a window frame.

beak molding
A molding ornamented with carved birds or fantastic animal-like heads or beaks.

billet molding
A common Norman or Romanesque molding formed by a series of circular cylinders, arranged alternately with notches in single or multiple rows.

bolection molding
A molding projecting beyond the surface of the work which it decorates, as that between a panel and the surrounding stiles and rails; often used to conceal a joint when the joining surfaces are at different levels.

cable molding
An ornamental molding formed like a cable showing twisted strands; the convex filling of the lower part of the flutes of classical columns.

calf's-tongue molding
A molding consisting of a series of pointed tongue-shaped elements all pointing in the same direction or toward a common center when around an arch.

cant molding
A square or rectangular molding with the outside face beveled.

cap molding
Trim at the top of a window or door; above the casing trim.

cavetto molding
A hollow member or round concave molding used in cornices and column bases, containing at least one quadrant of a circle in its profile.

chain molding
A molding carved with a representation of a chain.

corner bead
A vertical molding used to protect the external angle of two intersecting wall surfaces; a perforated metal strip used to strengthen and protect an external angle in plaster work or gypsum wallboard construction.

cove molding
A concave or canted interior corner molding, especially at the transition from the wall to a ceiling or floor.

cover molding
Any plain or molded wood strip covering a joint as between sections of paneling, or to cover a butt joint.

crenellated molding
Molding notched or indented to represent merlons and embrasures in fortifications.

crown molding
Any molding serving as a corona or otherwise forming the crowning or finishing member of a structure.

cyma molding
A molding with a profile of double curvature or ogee.

cyma recta molding
A molding of double curvature which is concave at the outer edge and convex at the inner edge.

cyma reversa molding
A molding of double curvature which is convex at the outer edge and concave at the inner edge.

cymatium molding
The crowning molding of a classical cornice, especially in the form of a cyma.

dovetail molding
A molding consisting of decorated fretwork in the form of dovetails.

drip molding
Any molding so formed and located as to act as a drip.

drop molding
A panel molding recessed below the surface of the surrounding stiles and rails.

egg-and-dart
An egg-shaped ornament alternating with a dart-like ornament, used to enrich ovolo and echinus moldings and also on bands.

fillet molding
A molding consisting of a narrow flat band, often square in section; the term is loosely applied to almost any rectangular molding, usually used in conjunction with other moldings or ornaments.

flush bead molding
A molding whose surface is on the same plane as that of the wood member or assembly to which it is applied.

Guilloche
An ornament in the form of two or more bands twisted together in a continuous series, leaving circular openings which are filled with round ornaments.

half-round molding
A convex strip or molding of semicircular profile.

hollow molding
A concave, often circular molding; a cavetto.

hollow square molding
A common molding consisting of a series of indented pyramidal shapes having a square base, found in Norman architecture.

hoodmold
The projecting molding of the architrave over a door or window, whether inside or outside; also called a dripstone.

indented molding
A molding with the edge toothed or indented in triangular tooth-like shapes.

lattice molding
A wood molding, rectangular in section and broad in relation to its projection, resembling the wood strips used in latticework.

medallion molding
A molding consisting of a series of medallions, found in the later examples of Norman architecture.

notched molding
An ornament produced by notching the edges of a band or fillet.

ovolo molding
A common convex molding consisting of a quarter circle in section.

pellet molding
Any small, round decorative projection; one of a series of small, flat disks or hemispherical projections.

quarter-round molding
A convex molding, with a projection that is exactly or nearly a quarter of a circle.

quirk bead molding
A molding containing a bead with a quirk on one side, as on the edge of a board.

quirked molding
A molding characterized by a sudden and sharp return from its extreme projection, or set-off and made prominent by a quirk running parallel to it.

raking molding
Any molding adjusted at a slant, rake, or ramp; any overhanging molding which has a rake or slope downward and outward.

reed molding
A small convex molding, usually one of several set close together to decorate a surface.

reticulated molding
A molding decorated with fillets interlaced to form a network or meshlike appearance.

roll molding
Any convex rounded molding, which has a cylindrical or partially cylindrical form.

rover molding
Any member used as a molding that follows the line of a curve.

scotia molding
A deep concave molding, especially one at the base of a column in classical architecture.

scroll molding
An ornamental molding consisting of a spiral design or a terminal similar to the volutes of the Ionic capital or the "S" curve on consoles.

square billet molding
A Norman molding consisting of a series of projecting cubes, with spaces between the cubes.

struck molding
A molding cut into rather than added to or planted onto another member.

sunk fillet molding
A molding slightly recessed behind the surface on which it is located; a fillet formed by a groove in a plane surface.

tresse molding
Flat or convex bandelets which are intertwined; especially such interlacing ornamentation used to adorn moldings.

wave moldings
A molding decorated with a series of stylized representations of breaking waves.

Monastery
A building complex of a monastic order.

Monolith
An architectural member such as an obelisk, the shaft of a column, consisting of a single stone.

Monolithic
Shapes usually formed of a single block of stone, or cast in one piece without construction joints; these are massive and uniform.

Monostyle
Having the same style of architecture throughout the structure; a single shaft applied to medieval pillars.

Monument
A stone, pillar, megalith, structure or building erected in memory of the dead, an event, or an action.

Monumental scale See Scale.

Moon gate See Gate.

Moorish arch See Arch.

Moorish architecture
Prevalent in Spain and Morocco, the style (500–900) was influenced by Mesopotamian brick and stucco techniques with frequent use of the horseshoe arch, along with Roman marble columns and limestone carved capitals. Vaults developed into highly complex ornate forms. Brick was used decoratively and structurally in combination with marble, with extensive use of stucco to build up the richly molded surfaces, painted with bright colors and sometimes gilded.

Mortar joints

bed joint
The horizontal joint between two masonry courses; one of the radial joints in an arch.

concave joint
A recessed masonry joint, formed in mortar by the use of a curved steel jointing tool; because of its curved shape it is very effective in resisting moisture.

flush joint
A masonry joint finished flush with the surface.

ground joint
A closely fitted joint in masonry, usually without mortar; a machined metal joint which fits tightly without packing or a gasket.

head joint
A vertical joint between two masonry units, perpendicular to the face of a wall.

raked joint
A joint made by removing the surface of mortar with a square-edged tool, while it is still soft; produces marked shadows and tends to darken the overall appearance of a wall; not a weather-tight joint.

rustic joint
In stone masonry, a deeply sunk mortar joint that has been emphasized by having the edges of the adjacent stones chamfered or recessed below the surface of the stone facing.

struck joint
A masonry joint from which excess mortar has been removed by a stroke of the trowel, leaving an approximately flush joint; a weather-struck joint.

tooled joint
Any masonry joint that has been prepared with a tool before the mortar in the joint has set rigidly.

troweled joint
A mortar joint finished by striking off excess mortar with a trowel.

v-shaped joint
A horizontal V-shaped mortar joint made with a steel jointing tool; very effective in resisting the penetration of rain.

weather-struck joint
A horizontal masonry joint in which the mortar is sloped outward from the upper edge of the lower brick, so as to shed water readily; formed by pressing the mortar inward at the upper edge of the joint.

Mortise and tenon joint See Joint.

Mosaic
A process of inlaying small pieces of stone, tile, glass or enamel into a cement or plaster matrix, making a pattern, design, or representational picture.

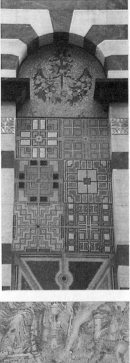

florentine mosaic
A kind of mosaic made with precious and semiprecious stones, inlaid in a surface of white or black marble or similar material, generally displaying elaborate floor patterns.

venetian mosaic
A type of terrazzo topping containing primarily large chips, with smaller chips filling in between.

Mosque
A Muslim house of worship.

Motif
A principal part or element repeated in an ornamental design.

Mouchette
Gothic tracery and derivatives, a typical small motif, pointed, elongated, and bounded by elliptical and ogee curves, a dagger motif with a curved axis.

Mozarabic architecture
A northern Spanish style (800–1400) built by Christian refugees from Moorish domination, characterized by the horseshoe arch and retaining all other Moorish features.

Mudejar architecture
A Spanish style (1200–1300) created by the Moors while under Christian domination, characterized by a fusion of Romanesque and Gothic styles but retaining some Islamic elements, such as the horseshoe arch.

Mullion
A dividing piece between the lights of windows, usually taking on the characteristics of the style of the building.

Multicentered arch   See **Arch.**

Multifoil   See **Foil.**

Multiple dwelling
A building for residential use which houses several separate family units.

139

Multistory frame
A building framework of more than one story in which loads are carried to the ground by a system of beams and columns.

Muntin
A secondary framing member to hold panes in a window, window wall, or glazed door; an intermediate vertical member that divides panels of a door.

Muqarnas
An original Islamic design involving various combinations of three-dimensional shapes featuring elaborate corbeling.

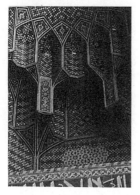

Museum
An institution for the assembly and public display of any kind of collection, especially one of rare or educational value.

Muslim architecture
In this style (600–1500) a new domed mosque was developed from the Christian basilica. There were many variations of the basic elements such as arches, domes, cross ribs, and crenellations. Surfaces are covered with an abundant geometric, floral and calligraphic decoration executed in stone, brick, stucco, wood and glazed tile.

Mutule
A sloping flat block on the soffit of the Doric cornice, usually decorated on the underside with rows of six guttae each; occurs over each triglyph and metope of the frieze.

Mycenaean architecture
The earliest phase (1600–1200 B.C.) was exemplified by masonry sidewalls and a timber roof. Monumental beehive-like tombs were constructed of superimposed layers of corbelled stones to create a parabolic vault. Stone-faced, inclined access passages led to the entrance, which had sloping jambs; overhead, a stone lintel supported a characteristic triangular panel with sculpture in relief.

N·n

Nara
A period in Japanese history (710–794) characterized by the adoption of Chinese culture and form of government, named after the first permanent capital and chief Buddhist center in ancient Japan.

Natural forms
Refers to those forms that include artificial foliage as well as derivations of the acanthus leaf, flowers and fruit festoons; also animal forms, such as the lion and eagle, and human forms, such as heads and figures.

Nave
The principal or central part of a church; by extension, both middle and side aisles of a church, from the entrance to the crossing of the chancel; that part of the church intended for the general public.

Neck
In the classical orders, the space between the bottom of the capital and the top of the shaft, which is usually marked by a sinkage or a ring of moldings.

Neoclassicism

A revival style (1900–1920) based primarily on Greek and to a lesser extent on Roman orders, producing symmetrically arranged buildings of monumental proportions. Colossal pedimented porticos were flanked by a series of pilasters. The arch was not used, and enriched moldings are rare. The preference was for simple geometric forms and smooth surfaces. The design was based on the assembly of separate volumes, each dedicated to a single function.

Neo-Expressionism

Structures which express continuity of form by sweeping curves characterize this style (1964–1975). These structures were primarily the result of using reinforced concrete to create smooth shapes and seamless soaring forms.

Neo-Formalism

A style (1964–1970) which combines the classical symmetrical forms and smooth wall surfaces with arches of precast concrete and decorative metal grilles, often delicate in appearance.

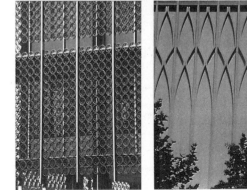

Neolithic Era

The last phase of the Stone Age (9000–8000 B.C.), characterized by the cultivation of crops and technically advanced stone implements.

Neopreme See **Plastic.**

Network

A system of subsidiary lines in a geometrical pattern that is usually composed of single squares or equilateral triangles.

New Brutalism

This style (1953–1965) was representative of buildings which expressed materials, structure and utilities honestly, in the tradition of Le Corbusier's beton brut; it featured rough, honest brickwork and exposed concrete imprinted with the grain of the wooden forms.

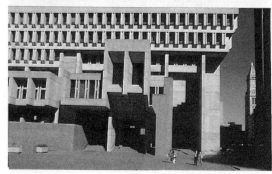

New Classicism

A final phase of Postmodernism (1982–) that led to a new form of Classicism, a freestyle version of the traditional language. It shares traditional assumptions of previous revivals, such as relating ideas to the past and using universal figures of representation as the design vocabulary. It combines two purist styles — Classicism and Modernism — and adds new forms based on new technologies and social usage. Previous rules of composition are not disregarded but rather extended and distorted. Among those identified with this style are James Stirling, Robert Venturi, Michael Graves, Hans Hollein, Charles Moore and Arata Isozaki.

New Classicism

New England Colonial style

A local style (1600–1700) characterized by a natural use of materials in a straightforward manner. The boxlike appearance is relieved by a prominent chimney and a sparse distribution of small casement-type windows. The characteristic shape, formed by extending the rear roof to a lower level than the front roof, was called a "saltbox." In larger structures the upper floor projected beyond the lower floor, creating an overhang called a jetty.

Newel

The central post or column which provides support for the inner edges of the steps in a circular staircase and around which the steps wind.

Newel cap

The terminal feature of a newel post often molded or turned in a decorative manner.

Newel post

A tall post at the head or foot of a stair, supporting the handrail, often ornamental.

Niche

A recess in a wall, usually semicircular at the back, terminating in a half-dome, or with small pediments supported on consoles; often used as a place for a statue.

Niche

angle niche
A niche formed at a corner of a building; common in medieval architecture.

Noncombustible
In building construction a material that will not ignite, burn, support combustion, or release flammable vapors when subjected to fire or heat.

Nonconforming
Said of any building or structure which does not comply with the requirements set forth in applicable code, rules, or regulations.

Non-load bearing wall   See **wall**

Norman architecture
A Romanesque form of architecture (1066–1180) that predominated in England from the Norman Conquest to the rise of the Gothic. It was plain and massive, with moldings confined to small features; archways were plain and capitals devoid of ornament. As the style advanced, greater enrichment was introduced, and later examples exhibit a profusion of ornament. Windows resemble small doors without mullions. Pillars were slender and channeled.

Notched molding   See **Molding.**

Nursing home
A building used for the lodging, boarding, and nursery care for patients of mental or physical incapacity, who require care and related medical services less intense than those given in a hospital.

Nylon   See **Plastic.**

O·o

Oak   See **Wood.**

Obelisk
A monumental four-sided stone shaft, either monolithic or jointed, tapering to a pyramidal top.

Oblique projection   see **Projection drawing**

Oblique section   see **Projection drawing**

Oblong
A right-angle plane figure with unequal pairs of sides; can approach the dimensions of a square on the one hand, or stretch out to express a band on the other.

Obscure glass   See **Glass.**

Observatory
A structure in which astronomical observations are carried out; a place such as an upper room which affords a wide view; a lookout.

Obsidian   See **Stone.**

Obtuse angle arch   See **Arch.**

Octagonal
Refers to those plane geometric figures containing eight equal sides and eight equal angles.

Octahedral
Forms that exhibit the characteristics of a regular polygon having eight sides.

Oculus
A roundel or bull's eye window opening, or an opening at the crown of a dome.

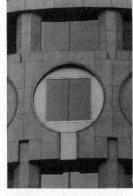

Ogee
A double curve resembling an "S" in shape, formed by the union of a convex and concave line.

ENCORE COMMUNITY CENTER

Ogee arch   See **Arch.**

Ogee molding   See **Molding.**

Ogee roof   See **Roof.**

Olmec architecture
This architecture (1200–500 B.C.) flourished in the tropical lowlands of the Mexican Gulf Coast, characterized by temple-pyramids and vast ceremonial centers.

One-point perspective   see **Perspective projection**

Onigawara
Ornamental tiles at the ends of the main roof ridge of a traditional Japanese structure, at the lower ends of the roof slopes, and at the corner ends. The most common is an ogre mask, from which it gets its name.

Onion dome   See **Dome.**

Opacity
Quality of being impenetrable by light, not reflecting light, or not transmitting light; neither transparent nor translucent.

Open cornice   See **Cornice.**

Open pediment   See **Pediment.**

Open stair   See **Stair.**

Open-timbered
Heavy timber work which is exposed and not concealed by sheathing, plaster, or other covering.

Open-timbered roof   See **Roof.**

Openwork
Any work characterized by perforations, especially of an ornamental nature.

Opera house
A theater intended primarily for the public performance of opera.

Operable transom
A panel of glass light above a door, which may be opened for ventilation.

Operable window   See **Window**.

Opposition
The state or position of being placed opposite another, or of lying in corresponding positions from an intervening space or object.

Orb
A plain circular boss, used as a decorative accent, where two or more ribs of a vault cross each other.

Organic architecture

Orchestration
To organize and combine harmoniously so as to achieve a desired or effective combination of form, color, and texture of materials.

Order
A logical and regular arrangement among the separate components or elements of a group; a unity of idea, feeling and form.

Orders
In classical architecture, a style of columns and capitals with their entablatures having standardized details. Greek orders are the Doric, Ionic, and Corinthian; the Romans added the Tuscan and the Composite.

Organic
Refers to forms that have a structure that perfectly fulfills their own functional requirements; intellectually integrated by a systematic connection and coordination of the parts to the whole.

Organic architecture
The principles of organic architecture (1985–) rely on the integration of form and function, in which the structure and appearance of a building is based on a unity of forms that stresses the integration of individual parts to the whole concept, relating it to the natural environment in a deliberate way, with all forms expressing the natural use of materials.

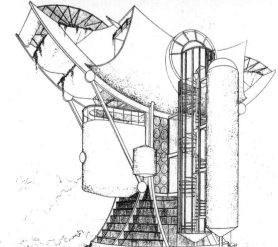

145

Organization

An arrangement of elements or interdependent parts with varied functions into a coherent and functioning entity.

centralized organization
Spaces gathered around or coming together at a large or dominant central area.

clustered organization
Spaces that are grouped, collected, or gathered closely together and related by proximity to each other.

embedded organization
A space incorporated as an integrated and essential part of a larger space.

grid-based organization
Spaces that are organized with references to a rectangular system of lines and coordinates.

interlocking organization
Two spaces interwoven or fit into each other so as to form an area of common space.

linear organization
Spaces that are extended, arranged, or linked along a line, path, or gallery.

linked organization
Two spaces that are joined or connected by a third intervening space.

radial organization
Spaces arranged like radii or rays from a central space or core.

Oriel window See **Window.**

Orientation
The placement of a structure on a site with regard to local conditions of sunlight, wind, drainage, and an outlook to specific vistas.

Orientation

Ornament
Anything that embellishes, decorates, or adorns a structure, whether used intentionally and integrated into the structure, or applied separately to enhance the building's form and appearance.

banderole ornament
A decorative representation of a ribbon or long scroll, often bearing an emblem or inscription.

cornucopia ornament
A goats horn overflowing with fruits, flowers and corn, signifying prosperity; a horn of plenty; any cone-shaped receptacle or ornament.

crocket ornament
In Gothic architecture and derivatives, an upward-oriented ornament, often vegetal in form, regularly spaced along sloping or vertical edges of emphasized features such as spires, pinnacles and gables.

fleur-de-lis ornament
A stylized three-petaled flower representing the French royal lily, tied by an encircling band, and used as an ornamental device in Late Gothic architecture and in later derivatives.

hip knob ornament
A finial or other similar ornament placed on the top of the hip of a roof or at the apex of a gable.

hollyhock ornament
A tall plant, widely cultivated for its showy spike of large variously colored flowers; used as an ornamental motif by Frank Lloyd Wright on the Barnsdall residence in Los Angeles.

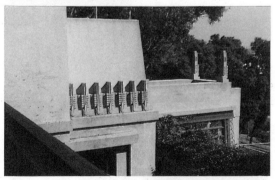

honeysuckle ornament
A common name for the anthemion, common in Greek decorative sculpture.

knot ornament
In medieval architecture, a bunch of leaves, flowers, or a similar ornament, such as bosses at the intersection of ribs, and bunches of foliage in capitals; an ornamental design resembling cords which are interlaced.

palmette ornament
An ornamental motif that is derived from a palm leaf.

scroll ornament
Ornamentation that consists of a spirally wound band or a band resembling a partially rolled scroll of paper; "S" scrolls are found in ornamental brackets, window and door surrounds, and in other ornamental bands.

tooth ornament
A decoration generally in the hollow of a Gothic molding consisting of four-leaved flowers, the centers of which project in a point.

Ornamental
Forms that adorn or embellish a surface or any other part of a structure.

Ornamental iron
Cast iron used for grilles, gates, finials, hardware and innumerable architectural accessories.

147

Ornamental metals
Bronze, brass, copper, aluminum and stainless steel, not used for major construction, but as infill materials, including copper panels, sheet aluminum, stainless steel, and baked enamel metal alloy panels.

Ornamentation
Any adjunct or detail used to adorn, decorate, or embellish the appearance or general effect of an object.

Orthographic projection see **Projection drawing**

Ottoman style
The phase of Turkish Islamic architecture (1350–1550), much influenced by Byzantine forms, under the rule of Ottoman sultans in the Balkans, Anatolia, and the Middle East.

Ottonian architecture
The pre-Romanesque round-arched style (960–1000) in Germany during the rule of the Ottonian emperors, characterized by the development of forms derived from Carolingian and Byzantine styles.

Outer string See **String.**

Outlooker
A member which projects beyond the face of a gable and supports the overhanging portion of a roof.

Oval
Resembling an egg in shape, ellipsoidal or elliptical; it is duocentric with a long and short axis.

Oval

Overdoor
A wall area directly above a doorway containing a panel ornamented with carvings or figures.

Overhang
The projection of an upper story or roof beyond the story immediately below.

Overhanging
Projecting or extending beyond the wall surface below.

Overlapping
Forms extending over and
covering part of an area or
surface that has a common
alignment; it may be slight
or significant, as long as
there is a common surface
between the elements.

Overlapping

Overlapping counterpoint See **Counterpoint.**

Ovolo molding See **Molding.**

Ovum
An egg-shaped ornamen-
tal motif, used in ornamental bands, found in classical
architecture and classical
revival styles.

Owl See **animal forms.**

Ox-eye window See **Window.**

P·p

Pagoda
A multistory shrinelike tower, originally a Buddhist monument crowned by a stupa. The stories may be open pavilions of wood with balconies and pent roofs of diminishing size with corbeled cornices.

Pai-lou See Gate.

Palazzo
In Italy, a palace or any impressive public building or private residence.

Paleolithic Era
The cultural period beginning with the first chipped stone tools, about 750,000 years ago, and continuing until the beginning of the Mesolithic era, about 15,000 years ago.

Palladian style
A style (1508–1580) named after Andrea Palladio, an Italian Renaissance architect, whose *Four Books of Architecture* set out the classic orders in detail, establishing the proportions between the various components in each one. He studied the Roman architect Vitruvius and the laws of harmonic proportions. His villas were an inspiration for many of the later country houses, especially in England.

Palladianism
A mode of building following strict Roman forms, particularly popular in England, as set forth in the publications of the Italian Renaissance architect Andrea Palladio (1508–1580).

Palladian motif
A door or window opening in three parts, divided by posts, featuring a round-headed archway flanked by narrow openings with a flat lintel over each side; the arched area rests on their flat entablatures.

Palm capital See Capital.

Palmette ornament See Ornament.

Pancharam
One of a number of miniature shrines located on the roof, cornices, or lintels of a Hindu temple, used as a decorative feature.

Panel
A portion of a flat surface recessed below the surrounding area, set off by moldings or some other distinctive feature.

Paneled door See Door.

Panel divider
A molding which separates two wood panels along their common edge.

Pantile
A roofing tile in the shape of an "s" laid on its side and overlapped in courses running up the slope of the roof.

Pantograph
A drafting instrument for copying drawings, plans, either at the same scale or at an enlarged or reduced scale.

Paper-mache
A material used for modelmaking composed principally of paper; prepared by pulping a mass of paper, sometimes adding glue to produce a dough-like consistency, and molding it into a desired form.

Papyriform capital See Capital.

Parabolic
Forms which resemble a parabola in outline or three-dimensional shape.

Parabolic arch See Arch.

Paraboloid roof   See **Roof**.

Paraline drawing   see **Projection drawing**

Parallel counterpoint   See **Counterpoint**.

Parallelogram
A quadrilateral having both pairs of the opposite sides parallel to each other.

Parapet
A low protective wall or railing along the edge of a roof, balcony, or similar structure; in an exterior wall, the part entirely above the roof.

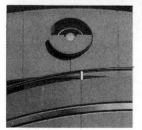

Parapet gutter
A gutter which is constructed behind a parapet wall.

Pargetting   See **Plaster**.

Parking garage
A garage for passenger vehicles only, exclusively for the purpose of parking or storing of automobiles and not for automobile repairs or service work.

Parquet
A flat inlay pattern of closely fitted pieces, usually geometrical, for ornamental flooring or wainscoting; often employing two or more colors or materials such as stone or wood.

Parthian architecture
The architecture (400 B.C.–200 A.D.) developed under Parthian rule in Iran and western Mesopotamia, combining classical with indigenous features.

Parti   See **Design drawing**.

Particle board   See **Wood products**.

Partition wall   See **Wall**.

Party wall   See **Wall**.

Passageway
A space connecting one area or room of a building with another.

Patera
A representation of a flat round or oval disk in friezes.

Patina
A greenish-brown crust produced by oxidation which forms on the surface of copper and bronze, often multi-colored and considered decorative; any thin oxide film which forms on a metal or other material.

Patio
An outdoor area, often paved and shaded, adjoining or enclosed by the walls or arcades of a house.

Pattern
The juxtaposition of repetitive elements in a design, organized so as to produce an arrangement of parts that are viewed as an unit; may occur at various scales and sizes.

Pattern

Pavement

Patterned glass See Glass.

Pavement
The durable surface of a sidewalk, or other outdoor area, such as a walkway or open plaza.

Pavilion

An open structure or small ornamental building, shelter or kiosk, usually detached, and used for specialized activities; it is often located as a terminal structure with a hipped roof, producing a pyramidal form.

Pavilion roof See **Roof**.

Paving tile See **Tile**.

Pebble wall masonry See **Masonry**.

Pedestal

A support for a column, urn, or statue, consisting of a base and a cap or cornice.

Pediment

A low-pitched triangular gable above a facade, or a smaller version over porticos above the doorway or above a window; a triangular gable end of the roof above the horizontal cornice, often with sculpture.

Pediment

brocken pediment
A pediment with its raking cornice split apart at the center, and the gap often filled with an urn, cartouche, or other ornament.

broken pediment

open pediment
A broken pediment.

round pediment
A rounded pediment, used ornamentally over a door or window.

Peg
A pointed pin of wood, metal, or any other material; used as a fastener.

Pegboard
A hard composition fiberboard material in sheet form, having regular rows of holes in it, through which hooks or pegs may be fastened.

Pellet molding See **Molding.**

Pendant
A hanging ornament or suspended feature on ceilings or vaults.

Pendentive

The curved triangular surface that results when the the top corner of a square space is vaulted so as to provide a circular base for a dome.

Pergola

A garden structure consisting of an open wooden-framed roof, often latticed and supported by regularly spaced posts or columns and often covered by climbing plants to shade a walk or passageway.

Pendentive bracketing

Corbeling in the general form of a pendentive; common in Moorish and Muslim architecture.

Pent roof See **Roof**.

Pentagonal

A plane figure with five equal sides and five equal angles, common in nature.

Penthouse

A structure on a flat-roofed building, occupying usually less than half the roof area.

Perforated

Forms that exhibit holes or a series of holes in a pattern; formed by combining elements to produce voids or through carving or casting materials containing pierced openings.

Peripteral

Surrounded on the perimeter by a single row of columns.

Peristyle

A row of columns around the outside of a building or around the inside of a courtyard.

Perpendicular style

The last and longest phase of Gothic architecture in England (1350–1550) was characterized by a vertical emphasis and elaborate fan vaults, displaying perpendicular tracery.

Perpendicular tracery   See **Tracery**

Perron

A formal terrace or platform, especially one centered on a gate or doorway; an outdoor flight of steps, usually symmetrical, leading to a terrace.

Persian architecture

Architecture (550–330 B.C.) developed under the kings who ruled ancient Persia during the Achaemenid dynasty, characterized by a synthesis of architectural elements from surrounding countries, such as Assyria, Egypt and Greece.

Persona

A mask of terra-cotta, stone or marble, designed to imitate the human face or the head of an animal, usually in the form of a grotesque; employed as an antic or as a gargoyle for discharging water.

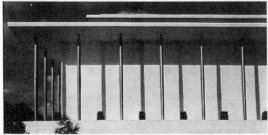

Persona

Perspective drawing

Any one of a variety of techniques for representing three-dimensional objects and spatial relationships on a two-dimensional surface in the same manner as they would appear to the eye.

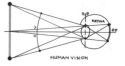

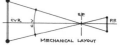

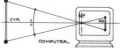

Perspective projection

A method of projection in which a three-dimensional object can be represented by projecting points upon a picture plane using straight lines converging at a fixed point representing the eye of the viewer.

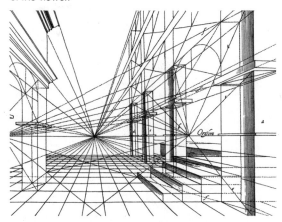

central visual axis
The sightline, which is perpendicular to the picture plane, indicating the direction in which the viewer is looking.

center of vision
A point representing the intersection of the central axis of vision and the picture plane in linear perspective drawing.

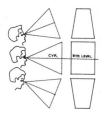

cone of vision
The field of vision radiating outwardly from the eye of the viewer in a more or less conical shape along the central visual axis.

ground line
A horizontal line representing the intersection of the ground plane and the picture plane.

ground plane
A horizontal plane of reference in linear perspective from which vertical measurements can be taken, usually it is the plane supporting the object depicted or the one on which the viewer stands.

horizon line
A horizontal line in linear perspective representing the intersection of the picture plane and a horizontal plane through the eye of the viewer.

measuring line
Any line coincident with or parallel to the picture plane, as the ground line, on which measurements can be taken.

one-point perspective
A perspective of an object with a principal face parallel to the picture plane; all horizontal lines parallel to the picture plane remain as is, and all other horizontal lines converge to a selected vanishing point.

one-point perspective

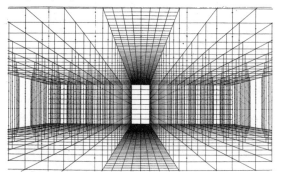

picture plane
An imaginary transparent plane, coexistent with the drawing surface, on which the image of a three-dimensional object is projected, and upon which all lines can be measured and drawn to exact scale.

station point
A fixed point in space representing a single eye of the viewer.

three-point perspective
A perspective of an object with all faces oblique to the picture plane; the three sets of parallel lines converge to three different vanishing points; one left, one right, and one above or below the horizon line.

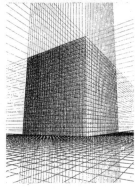

157

two-point perspective
A perspective of an object having two faces oblique to the picture plane; the vertical lines parallel to the picture plane remain vertical, and two horizontal sets of parallel lines oblique to the picture plane appear to converge to two vanishing points - one to the left, and one to the right.

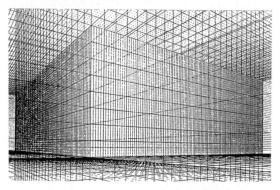

vanishing point
A point towards which receding parallel lines appear to converge, located at the point where a sight line parallel to the set of lines intersects the picture plane.

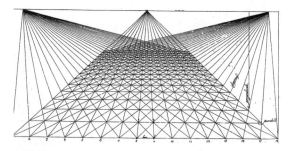

Piazza
A public open space or square surrounded by buildings.

Picture plane see **Perspective projection**

Picture window See **Window.**

Pier
A free-standing support for an arch, usually composite in section and thicker than a column, but performing the same function; also, a thickened part of a wall to provide lateral support or bear concentrated loads.

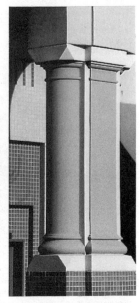

Pier buttress
A pier which receives the thrust of a flying buttress.

158

Pierced work

Decoration which consists mainly of perforations. A nonbearing masonry wall in which an ornamental pierced effect is achieved by alternating rectangular or other shaped blocks with open spaces.

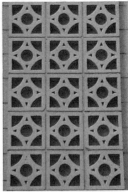

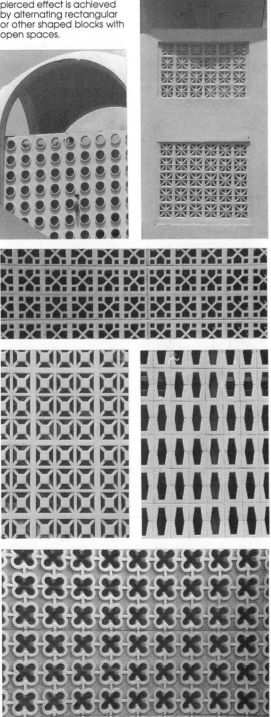

Pierced work

Pilaster

A partial pier or column, often with a base, shaft and capital, that is embedded in a flat wall and projects slightly; may be constructed as a projection of the wall itself.

Pilaster

Pilaster face

grouped pilaster
Three or more closely spaced pilasters forming a group, often on one pedestal.

Pilaster face
The front surface of a pilaster, parallel to the wall.

Pilaster mass
An engaged pier built up with the wall, usually without a capital or base.

Pilaster side
The form of the side surface of a pilaster perpendicular to the wall.

Pilaster strip
A slender pier of minimal projection.

Pillar
A column or post supporting an arch or other superimposed load. Clustered or compound pillars consist of a central shaft with smaller shafts grouped around it.

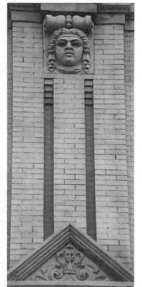

Pilotis
The free-standing columns, posts, or piles which support a building, raising it above an open ground level.

Pin
A peg or bolt of wood, metal, or any other material, which is used to fasten or hold something in place, or serve as a point of support.

Pine See **Wood.**

Pinnacle
An apex or small turret that usually tapers towards the top as a termination to a buttress.

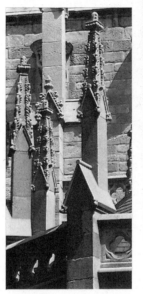

Pinwheel
Shapes that are fixed at the center with identical radiating arms, either angular or curvilinear, and repeated any number of times within the circumference of the circle from which they are generated.

Pise'
A building whose walls are made of compressed earth, usually stiff clay formed and rammed into a movable framework; the building material itself; i.e., stiff earth or clay, rammed until firm to form walls and floors.

Pitch-faced masonry See **Masonry.**

Pitched roof See **Roof.**

Pivoted door See **Door.**

Pivoting window See **window.**

Plaid
A pattern created by regularly spaced bands at right angles to one another; the resultant checkered effects vary widely, depending on the relationship and intervals between lines and bands.

Plan
A two-dimensional graphic representation of the design, location, and dimensions of the project, or parts thereof, viewed in a horizontal plane from above.

Plan

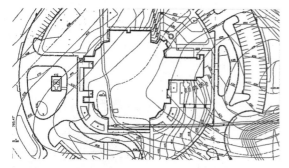

Plane

The simplest kind of two-dimensional surface, generated by the path of a straight line and defined by its length and width; the fundamental property of a plane is its shape and surface characteristics.

Planning

The process of studying the layout of spaces within a building or other facility, or installations in open spaces, in order to develop the general scheme of a building or group of buildings.

Planning grid

An arrangement of one or more sets of regularly spaced parallel lines, with the sets at right angles or other selected angles to each other, and used like graph paper to assist with modular planning.

Planter

A permanent, ornamental container to receive planted pots or boxes, often nonmovable and integral with the finish of a building.

Plaque

A tablet, often inscribed, added to or set into a surface on the exterior or interior wall.

Plaque

Plaster
A mixture of lime or gypsum, sand, portland cement and water produces a pastelike material which can be applied to the surfaces of walls and ceilings, and which later sets to form a hard surface.

daubing
A rough coating of plaster given to a wall by throwing plaster against it.

intonaco
The fine finish coat of plaster made with white marble dust to receive a fresco painting.

pargetting
A decorative feature in which flat wet plaster is ornamented by patterns either scratched or molded into it, sometimes decorated with figures either in low relief or indented.

rendering
A coat of plaster directly on an interior wall or stucco on an exterior wall; a perspective or elevation drawing of a project or portion thereof with artistic delineation of materials, shades, and shadows.

scagliola
Plaster work that imitates stone, in which mixtures of marble dust, sizing, and various pigments are laid in decorative figures routed into the surface.

shikkui
A plaster, mortar, stucco, or whitewash, made from a mixture of lime and clay and having the consistency of glue, used in traditional Japanese construction.

Plastic
Any of the various synthetic complex organic compounds produced by polymerization; can be molded, extruded, or cast into various shapes or drawn into filaments and used as fibers.

acrylic fiber
A synthetic polymer fiber.

fiberglass
The generic term for a material consisting of extremely fine filaments of glass that are mixed with a resin to give the desired form in a mold. Layers of this combination are laid or sprayed into the mold.

nylon
A class of thermoplastics characterized by extreme toughness, strength, and elasticity and capable of being extruded into filaments, fibers and sheets.

plexiglass
Used for windows and lighting fixtures.

polyethelene
A tough, light, flexible thermoplastic used in the form of sheeting and film for packaging, dampproofing, and as a vapor barrier.

polystyrene plastic
A hard, tough, stable thermoplastic that is easily colored, molded, expanded, or rolled into sheeting.

vinyl
Any of various tough, flexible plastics made from polyvinyl resin.

Plate
In wood frame construction, a horizontal board connecting and terminating posts, joists, or rafters; a timber laid horizontally on the ground to receive other timbers or joists.

Plate glass   See **Glass.**

Plate tracery   See **Tracery.**

Plateresque architecture
The richly decorative style of the Spanish Renaissance in the 16th century; also referred to as Isabelline architecture, after Queen Isabella I (1474–1504).

Platform
A raised floor or terrace, open or roofed; a stair landing.

Playhouse
A place of assembly for dramatic presentations; a small building serving children as a make-believe home.

Plaza
An open square or marketplace having one or more levels, approached in various ways by avenues, stairs, streets, or a combination.

Plexiglass See **Plastic**.

Plinth
A square or rectangular base for column, pilaster, or door framing to support a statue or memorial; a solid monumental base, often ornamented with moldings, bas-reliefs, or inscriptions.

Plinth block
A flat, plain member at the base of a pillar, column, pedestal or statue.

Plot
A parcel of land consisting of one or more lots or portions thereof, which is described by reference to a recorded plot by survey.

Plug-in architecture
A new type of architecture (1964–1970) proposed by the group Archigram. It consisted of a basic structure to contain transportation and communication services and a series of separate units — domestic environments, shops, and leisure activities — that are plugged in to a central module.

Plumbing system
The combination of supply and distribution pipes for hot water, cold water, and gas and for removing liquid wastes in a building which includes: the water-supply distribution pipes; fixtures and traps; the soils, waste, and vent pipes; the building drain and building sewer; storm-drainage pipes; and all connections within or adjacent to the building.

Plywood See **Wood products**.

Pneumatic architecture
A term referring to a style (1850–1880) of structures that are air-inflated, air-supported, and air-controlled. Structures generally consist of curved forms, domes or half cylinders. Their rounded forms are organic and responsive to the technology which utilizes fabric and cables supported from within by air pressure.

Pocket door See **Door**.

Podium
Any elevated platform; the high platform on which Roman temples were generally placed; a low step-like projection from a wall or building, intended to form a raised platform for placing objects.

Point
The smallest unit in a composition, depending on the scale of the work; it may be composed of straight lines and arcs, free forms (flowing and curvilinear), or a combination.

Pointed arch See **Arch**.

Pointed work
The rough finish which is produced by a pointed tool on the face of a stone.

Pointing
In masonry, the final treatment of joints by the troweling of mortar or a putty-like filler into the joints; the material with which the joints are filled.

Polygonal
Forms characteristic of a closed plane figure having three or more straight sides.

Polychromatic
Having or exhibiting a variety of colors.

Polychromy
The practice of decorating architectural elements or sculpture in a variety of colors.

Polyethelene See **Plastic.**

Polygonal masonry See **Masonry.**

Polyhedron
A solid geometric figure bounded by plane faces.

Polystyrene See **Plastic.**

Pop architecture
A style (1962–1974) which refers to structures that symbolically represent objects or fantastic designs for vast sculptures on an architectural scale or any architecture produced more as metaphor than building.

Porcelain enamel
A glassy metal oxide coating bonded to a metal panel at an extremely high temperature, and baked onto steel panels for large architectural applications. It is a very durable material, and is scratch resistant.

Porch
A roofed entrance, either incorporated in a building or as an applied feature on the exterior.

Portal
An entrance, gate, or door to a building or courtyard, often decorated, it marks the transition from the public exterior to the private interior space.

Porte-cochere
A carriage porch; a doorway large enough to let a vehicle pass from the street to a parking area.

Porthole
A small window, usually circular, in a ship's side, or on an exterior part of a structure.

165

Portico
A range of columns or arches in front of a building, often merged into the facade, including a covered walkway of which one or more sides are open; It includes every kind of covered ambulatory.

Post
Any stiff, vertical upright, made of wood, stone, or metal, used to support a superstructure or provide a firm point of lateral attachment.

angle post
The corner post in half-timbered construction.

crown post
Any vertical member in a roof truss, especially a king post.

king post
A vertical member extending from the apex of the inclined rafters to the tie beam between the rafters at the lower ends of a truss, as well as in a roof.

queen post
One of the two vertical supports in a queen-post truss.

Post-and-beam
A type of framing in which horizontal members are supported by a vertical post rather than by a bearing wall, or a system of arches and vaults.

Post-and-lintel construction
A type of construction characterized by the use of vertical columns, posts and a horizontal beam, or lintel to carry a load over an opening, in contrast to structural systems employing arches or vaults.

Postern
A minor often inconspicuous entry; a small door or gate near a larger one.

Post office
An office or building where letters and parcels are received and sorted, and from where they are distributed and dispatched to various destinations.

166

Postmodernism

A reaction against the International style and Modernism was evidenced in this style (1980–). It reintroduced ornament and decorative motifs to building design, often in garish colors and illogical juxtaposition. It is an eclectic borrowing of historical details from several periods, but unlike previous revivals is not concerned with scholarly reproduction. Instead, it is a light-hearted compilation of aesthetic symbols and details, often using arbitrary geometry, and with an intentional inconsistency of scale. The most prevalent aspect is the irony, ambiguity, and contradiction in the use of architectural forms. Those connected with the beginning of this movement include Aldo Rossi, Stanley Tigerman, Charles Moore, Michael Graves, Robert Krier, and Terry Farrell.

Prairie style

A style (1900–1940) that is typical of the low horizontal house associated mostly with the work of Frank Lloyd Wright and his followers. Horizontal elements were emphasized in these one- or two-story houses, built with brick or timber covered with stucco. The central portion rising above the flanking wings was separated by clerestory windows. The eaves of the low pitched roof extend well beyond the wall. A large chimney is located at the axis of intersecting roof planes. Casement windows are grouped into horizontal bands continuing around the corners. Exterior walls are highlighted by dark wood strips against a lighter stucco finish or by a coping of smooth stucco at the top of brick walls.

Precast concrete See **Concrete.**

Prefabrication

The manufacture of standardized units or components, usually at a mill or plant away from the site, for quick assembly and erection on the job site.

Prehistoric Era

The era before written or recorded human events, knowledge of which is gathered through archaeological investigations, discoveries and research.

Presentation drawing   See **Design drawing**.

Prestressed concrete   See **Concrete**.

Prismatic

Characteristic of a solid figure in which the two ends are similar and parallel figures with parallelograms for sides; used extensively in space frames covering open areas or large atrium areas.

Profile

An outline of a form or structure seen or represented from the side, or one formed by a vertical plane passed through an object at right angles to one of its main horizontal dimensions.

Progression

A gradual increase in the size or shape of a form or design, keeping the same basic theme or idea.

Progress schedule

A diagram, graph, or other pictorial or written schedule showing proposed and actual times of starting and completion of the various elements of the work.

Projecting window   See **Window**.

Projection

Any component, member, or part which juts out from a building; in masonry construction, stones or bricks which are set forward of the general wall surface to provide a rugged or rustic appearance.

Projection drawing

The process or technique of representing a three-dimensional object by projecting all its points by straight lines, either parallel or converging to a picture plane.

axonometric projection
The orthographic projection of a three-dimensional object inclined to the picture plane in such a way that its three principal axes can be drawn to scale but diagonal and curve lines appear distorted.

cutaway
A drawing or model having an outer section removed to display the interior space.

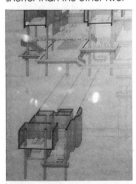

dimetric projection
An axonometric projection of a three-dimensional object to the picture plane in such a way that two of its principal axes are equally foreshortened, and the third appears longer or shorter than the other two.

exploded view
A drawing that shows the individual parts of a structure or construction separately but indicates their proper relationship to each other and to the whole.

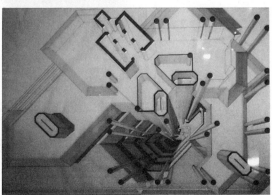

isometric projection
An axonometric projection of a three-dimensional object is created by having its principal faces equally inclined to the picture plane so that its three principal axes are all equally foreshortened.

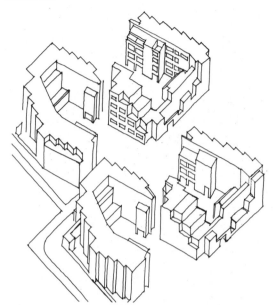

longitudinal section
An orthographic projection of a section made by cutting through the longest axis of an object.

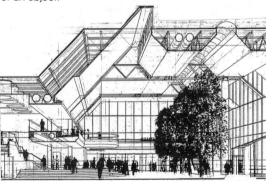

oblique projection
A method of projection in which a three-dimensional object, having one principal face parallel to the picture plane, is represented by projecting parallel lines at some angle other than ninety degrees.

oblique section
An orthographic projection of a section made by cutting with a plane that is neither parallel nor perpendicular to the long axis of an object.

orthographic projection
A method of projection in which a three-dimensional object is represented by projecting lines perpendicular to a picture plane.

169

paraline drawing
Any of various single-view drawings characterized by parallel lines remaining parallel to each other rather than converging as in linear perspective.

section
An orthographic projection of an object or structure as it will appear if cut through by an intersecting plane to expose its internal configuration.

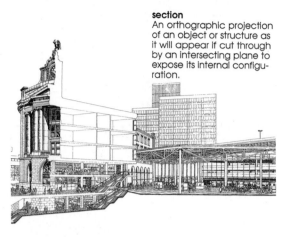

transverse section
An orthographic projection of a section made by cutting through an object along the shortest axis.

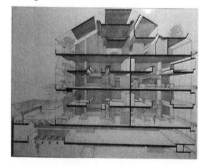

trimetric projection
An axonometric projection of a three-dimensional object inclined to the picture plane in such a way that all three principal axes are foreshortened at a different rate.

Promenade
A suitable place for walking for pleasure, as a mall.

Proportion
The ratio of one part to another, or its relationship to the whole; a comparison of parts as to size, length, width, and depth.

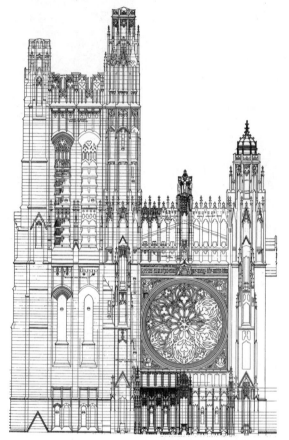

Propylaeum
The monumental gateway to a sacred enclosure; specifically, the elaborate gateway to the Acropolis in Athens.

Propylon

A monumental gateway, usually between two towers, in ancient Egyptian architecture. One or a series stood in front of the actual entrance or pylon of most temples or other important buildings.

Prostyle

Having a portico featuring columns at the exterior front of a building only.

Pseudoperipteral

A classical temple or other building which has columns all the way around; those on the flanks and rear are engaged rather than freestanding.

Public housing

Low-cost housing, owned, sponsored, or administered by a municipal or other government agency.

Pueblo

A communal dwelling and defensive structure of the Pueblo Indians of the Southwestern United States, built of adobe or stone, typically multistoried, and terraced, with entry through the flat roofs by ladder.

Pueblo style

A style (1905–1940) characterized by battered walls, rounded corners, and flat roofs with rounded ends of projecting roof beams. Windows had straight heads set deep into the walls. The second and third floors are terraced, resembling the Indian pueblos of the southwest.

Purlin

A piece of timber laid horizontally on the principal rafters of a roof to support the common rafters on which the roof covering is laid.

Putti

A decorative sculpture or painting representing chubby, usually naked infants, used in Renaissance architecture and classical derivatives.

Putti

Pylon

A monumental gateway in the form of a truncated pyramid or other vertical shaft marking the entrance approach to a structure.

Pyramid
A polyhedron with a polygonal base and triangular faces meeting at a single common apex.

Pyramidal roof See Roof.

Q·q

Quadrafron capital See Capital.

Quadrafrons
Having four fronts or faces looking in four directions.

Quadrangle
A rectangular courtyard or grassy area enclosed by buildings, most often used in conjunction with academic or civic building groupings.

Quadratura
In Baroque interiors and derivatives, painted architecture, often continuing into the three-dimensional trim, executed by specialists in calculated perspective.

Quarry faced masonry See Masonry.

Quarter-round molding See Molding.

Quartrafoil See Foil.

Quartzite See Stone.

Queen Anne arch
An arch over the triple opening of the Venetian or Palladian window, flat over the narrow side lights, round over the larger central opening.

Queen post See Post

Quirk
An indentation separating one element from another, as between moldings.

Quirk bead molding See Molding.

Quirked molding See Molding.

Quoin
One of a series of stones or bricks used to mark or visually reinforce the exterior corners of a building; often through a contrast of size, shape, color or material, which may be imitated in non-load-bearing material.

Quoin

rustic quoin
A quoin treated with sunken joints, with its face generally roughened and raised above the surface of the masonry.

Quoin header
A quoin which serves as a header in the face of a wall and a stretcher in the face of the return wall.

Quoining
Any members which form a quoin.

R·r

Radial
Forms radiating from or converging to a common center, or developing symmetrically about a central point.

Radial dome See Dome.

Radial organization See Organization.

Radial symmetry See Symmetry.

Rafter
One of a series of inclined members which supports the sheathing to which a roof covering is fixed.

hip rafter
A rafter located at the junction of the sloping sides of a hip roof.

jack rafter
Any rafter shorter than the full length of the sloping roof, such as one beginning or ending at a hip or valley.

valley rafter
In a roof framing system, the rafter in the line of the valley; connects the ridge to the wall plate along the meeting line of two inclined sides of a roof which are perpendicular to each other.

Rafter plate
A plate which supports the lower end of rafters and to which they are fixed.

173

Rail

A bar of wood or other material passing from one post or support to another support; a horizontal piece in the frame or paneling, as in a door rail or in the framework of a window sash.

Railing

Any open construction or rail used as a barrier, composed of one or a series of horizontal rails supported by spaced upright balusters.

Rainproof

Constructed, protected, or treated to prevent rain from entering a building.

Raised panel

A panel whose center portion is thicker than the edges or projects above the surrounding frame or wall surface.

Raised panel

Raked mortar joint   See Joint.

Raking bond   See Bond.

Raking coping   See Coping.

Raking cornice   See Cornice.

Raking molding   See Molding.

Rampant arch   See Molding.

Rampant vault   See Vault.

Random ashlar masonry   See Masonry.

Ratio

A relation in magnitude, quantity, or degree between two or more similar things.

Rear arch   See Arch.

Recessed

Forms created by indentations or small hollows in an otherwise plain surface or straight line; can be angular, rectilinear or curvilinear.

Recessed arch See Arch.

Record drawings
Construction drawings revised to show significant changes made during the construction process, usually based on marked-up prints, drawings, and other data furnished by the contractor to the architect.

Rectangle
A plane four-sided parallelogram with four right angles; may be nearly square or stretched out to be nearly a band.

Rectilinear
Forming, formed by, or characterized by straight lines.

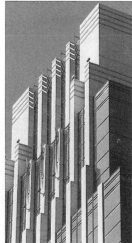

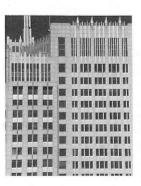

Rectilinear style
Similar to Perpendicular style; characterized by perpendicular tracery and intricate stonework.

Redwood See Wood.

Reed molding See Molding.

Reflection
The action on the part of surfaces of throwing back rays of light or sound falling upon them.

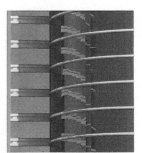

Reflection

Reflective glass See Glass.

Regence style
The decorative and elegant Rococo style (1715–1723) flourishing under the regency of Philip of Orleans during the rule of Louis XV.

Regency style
A colorful neoclassical style, often combined with oriental motifs (1811–1820), prevalent in England during the reign of George IV, characterized by close imitation of ancient Greek and Roman, Gothic, and ancient Egyptian forms.

Regula
In the Doric entablature, one of a series of short fillets beneath the taenia, each corresponding to a triglyph above.

Regular rhythm See Rhythm.

Reinforced concrete
Concrete masonry construction, in which steel reinforcement is embedded in such a manner that the two materials act together in resisting forces.

Reinforcing bar
A steel bar used in concrete construction that provides additional strength; the bars are deformed with patterns made during the rolling process.

Relief
Carved or embossed decoration of a figure or form, raised above the background plane from which it is formed.

alto-relievo
Sculptural relief work in which the figures project more than half their thickness from the base surface.

bas-relief
Sculptural decoration in low relief, in which none of the figures or motifs are separated from their background, projecting less than half their true proportions from the wall or surface. When the projection is equal to half the true proportion, it is called mezzo-relievo; when more than half, it is alto relievo. Double-aspect sculpture is halfway between relief and sculpture-in-the-round.

A MIDSOMMER NIGHTS DREA

THREE   ELEVEN

cavo-relievo
Relief which does not project above the general surface upon which it is carved.

analglyph
An embellishment carved in low relief.

diaglyph
A relief engraved in reverse,
an intaglio; a sunken relief.

glyph
A sculptured pictograph; a groove channel, usually vertical,
intended as an ornament.

high Relief
Sculptural relief work in
which the figures project
more than half their thickness from the base.

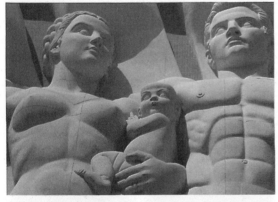

in cavetto
The reverse of relief, differing from intaglio in that the designs
are impressed into plaster or clay.

mezzo-relievo
Casting, carving, or em-
bossing in moderate relief,
intermediate between bas-
relief and high relief.

stiacciato
In very low relief, as if a bas-
relief had been pressed
even flatter.

stiacciato

sunk relief
Relief in which the highest point of the forms does not project above the general surface from which it is modeled; also called cavo-relievo.

Relieving arch See Arch.

Renaissance architecture

An architecture (1420–1550) which developed during the re-birth of classical art and learning in Europe and evolved through several periods into classicism. It was initially characterized by the use of the classical orders, round arches and symmetrical proportions. It represented a return to the models of Graeco-Roman antiquity, and was based on regular order, symmetry, and a central axis with grandiose plans and impressive facades. Silhouettes were clean and simple, with flat roofs replacing Gothic spires. Walls of large dressed masonry blocks gave buildings an imposing sense of dignity and strength. Gothic verticality was replaced with an emphasis on horizontality. Semicircular arches appeared over doors and windows and in freestanding arcades. Columns were used decoratively on facades and structurally in porticos, and ornamentation was based on pagan or classical mythological subjects.

Renaissance Revival style

A revival style (1840–1890) characterized by a studied formalism. Symmetrical compositions are reminiscent of early sixteenth century Italian elements. Ashlar masonry is accented with rusticated quoins, architrave framed windows, and doors supporting entablatures or pediments. A belt or string course may divide the ground or first floor from the upper story. Small square windows indicate the top story.

Render   See Plaster.

Rendering   See Design drawing.

Repetition

The recurrence of rhythmic patterns, forms or accents, separated by spaces of repeated formal elements or different forms.

Repose

Harmony in the arrangement of parts or colors that is restful to the eye.

Respond

A pier or pilaster projecting from a wall as a support for an arch at the end of an arcade.

Retaining wall   See Wall.

Reticulated

Refers to surfaces that are marked with lines, resembling or forming a network of squares arranged on the diagonal.

Reticulated molding   See Molding

Reticulated tracery   See Tracery.

Reticulated Work

Masonry constructed with diamond-shaped stones or square stones placed diagonally or crossing in a network.

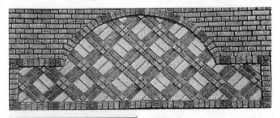

Return

The continuation of a molding, projection, member or cornice, in a different direction, usually at right angles.

Reveal
The visible side of an opening for a window or doorway between the framework and outer surface of the wall; where the opening is not filled with a door or window, the whole thickness of the wall.

Revival architecture
The use of older styles in new architectural movements, most often referring to the Gothic, Roman, Egyptian, Etruscan, Greek, Colonial, or revival styles of the 18th and 19th century.

Revolving door See Door.

Rhythm
Any kind of movement characterized by the regular occurrence of elements, lines, shapes and forms; the flow of movement shown by light and heavy accents, similar to recurring musical beats.

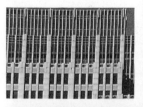

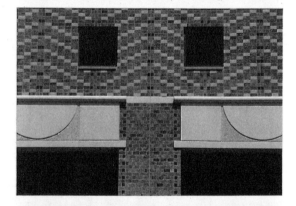

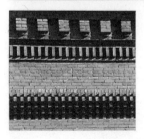

Rib
A curved structural member supporting any curved shape or panel; a molding which projects from the surface and separates the various roof or ceiling panels.

180   **Ribbed arch** See Arch.

Ribbed fluting
Flutes alternating with fillets.

Ribbed vault See Vault.

Ribbing
An assemblage or arrangement of ribs, as timberwork sustaining a vaulted ceiling.

Ribbon window See Window.

Richardsonian style
Named for Henry Hobson Richardson, this style (1870–1900) featured a straightforward treatment of stone, broad roof planes and a select grouping of door and window openings. It also featured a heavy, massive appearance with a simplicity of form and rough masonry. The effect is based on mass, volume, and scale rather than decorative detailing, except on the capitals of columns. The entry includes a large arched opening without columns or piers for support.

Ridge
The horizontal lines at the junction of the upper edges of two sloping roof structures.

Ridgebeam
A horizontal beam at the upper edge of the rafters, below the ridge of the roof.

Ridgeboard
A longitudinal member at the apex of a roof which supports the upper ends of the rafters.

Ridgecap
Any covering such as metal, wood, or shingles used to cover the ridge of a roof.

Ridge course
The last or top course of roofing tiles, roll roofing, or shingles.

Ridge roll
A wood strip, rounded on top, which is used to finish the ridge of a roof, often covered with lead sheathing; a metal or tile covering which caps the ridge of a roof.

Ridge tile See Tile.

Rigid arch See Arch.

Rigid frame
A structural framework in which all columns and beams are roughly connected; there are no hinged joints and the angular relationship between beam and column members are maintained under load.

Rigid frame

Rinceau
An ornamental band of undulant and curving plant motifs, found in classical architecture.

Ring stone
One of the stones of an arch which shows on the face of the wall or at the end of the arch; one of the voussoirs of the face forming the archivolt.

Rio Bec style
A style of Mayan architecture (550–900) that was transitional between that of sites at Tikal and at Uxmal; it was characterized by lavishly decorated structures flanked by soaring temple pyramids with steeply raked steps.

Riprap
Irregularly broken and random-sized large pieces of quarry rock used for foundations; a foundation or parapet of stones thrown together without any attempt at regular structural arrangements.

Riser See Step.

Rocaille
A small ornament combining forms based on water-worn rocks, plants and shells, characteristic of the 18th century Rococo period, especially during the reign of Louis XV.

Rock-cut
Said of a temple or tomb excavated in natural rock; usually represents an architectural front with dark interior chambers, of which sections are supported by masses of stone left in the form of solid pillars.

Rock rash
A patchwork applique of oddly shaped stone slabs used on edges as a veneer, often further embellished with small cobbles or geodes.

Rockwork
Quarry-faced masonry; any stonework in which the surface is left irregular and rough.

Rococo style
A style of architecture and decoration (1720–1790), primarily French in origin, representing the final phase of the Baroque. It was characterized by a profuse, semi-abstract ornamentation of shell work and foliage. It was associated with lightness, swirling forms, flowing lines, ornate stucco work, arabesque ornament, and the blending of separate members into a single molded volume.

Roll molding   See Molding.

Roll-up door   See door.

Rolling door   See Door.

Roman arch   See Arch.

Roman architecture
An architecture (300 B.C.–365 A.D.) influenced by the Etruscans, combining the use of the arch with Greek columns. The invention of concrete led to a system of vaulting and the development of the dome to roof a circular area, demonstrating sophisticated engineering skills. The pilaster was used decoratively on walls instead of half-columns. Colonnades and arcades were both in use, and occur one above the other at times. Doorway headers were both square and semicircular and became decorative features of importance in the exterior design of large public buildings. Window headers were generally semicircular. Orders were sometimes superimposed, and pedestals were developed to give the column additional height. The Romans relied on the abundant carving on their moldings rather than on the contours. Marble, granite and alabaster were the primary facing materials, as well as stucco and mosaics. The emphasis was on monumental public buildings, reflecting the grandeur of the empire. Many had sophisticated building services, such as plumbing, heating and water supply. On an urban scale the Romans also produced an impressive array of planning elements: formal axial planning with whole communities and towns constructed on a grid plan were typical.

Romanesque architecture

The style (800–1180) emerged from Roman and Byzantine elements, characterized by massive articulated wall structures, semicircular arches and vaults. It showed an evolution of stone vaulting and of the rib method of construction. It was characterized by heavy masonry construction, sparse ornament, smooth plain walls, with decoration derived from the structure. It also featured thick molded piers, assembled from small stones individually carved to fit.

Romanesque Revival style

A style (1840–1900) characterized by monochromatic brick or stone buildings, highlighted by semicircular arches over window and door openings. The arch was also used decoratively to enrich corbel tables along the eaves and courses marking horizontal divisions. The arches and capitals of columns are carved with geometrical medieval moldings. Facades are flanked by polygonal towers and covered with various roof shapes.

Romanesque Revival style

Rood
A large crucifix set above the chancel entrance.

Rood arch
The central arch in a rood screen.

Rood beam
A horizontal beam across the chancel to support the screen

Rood loft
A gallery in which the rood is kept.

Rood screen
A carved wood or stone separating the nave and chancel.

Rood spire
A spire over the crossing of the nave and transepts.

Rood stairs
Access to a rood loft.

Rood tower
A tower at the crossing and above the rood.

Roof

The external covering on the top of a building, usually of wood shingles, slates, or tiles on pitched slopes, or a variety of built-up membranes for flat roofs.

barrel roof

A roof of semicylindrical section; capable of spanning long distances, parallel to the axis of the cylinder.

bell roof

A roof whose cross section is shaped like a bell.

curb roof

A pitched roof that slopes away from the ridge in two successive planes, as in a gambrel or mansard roof.

flat roof
A roof having no slope, or one with only a slight pitch so as to drain rainwater; a roof with only sufficient slope to effect drainage.

gable roof
A roof having a gable at one or both ends; a roof sloping downward in two opposite directions from a central ridge, so as to form a gable at each end.

gambrel roof
A roof which has two pitches on each side.

hip roof
A roof which slopes upward from all four sides of a building, requiring a hip rafter at each corner.

mansard roof
A roof with a steep lower slope and a flatter upper slope on all sides, either of convex or concave shape.

ogee roof
A roof whose section is an ogee.

open-timbered roof
A roof construction in which there is no ceiling so that the rafters and roof sheathing are visible from below.

pavilion roof
A roof hipped equally on all sides, so as to have a pyramidal form; a similar roof having more than four sides, a polygonal roof.

pent roof
A small sloping roof, the upper end of which butts against a wall of a house, usually above the first-floor window; if carried completely around the house, it is called a skirt roof.

pitched roof
A roof having one or more slopes, surfaces.

pyramidal hipped roof
Same as a pavilion roof.

sawtooth roof
A roof system having a number of small parallel roof surfaces with a profile similar to the teeth in a saw; usually the steeper side is splayed and faces north; usually asymmetrical with the shorter slope glazed.

shed roof
A roof shape having only one sloping plane.

skirt roof
A false roof between stories of a building.

stepped roof
A roof constructed of stones which are arranged in a stair-stepped fashion, diminishing towards the top in a peak.

suspended roof
One whose load is carried by a number of cables which are under tension from columns or posts that are in compression and that transmit the loads to the ground.

thatched roof
A roof made of straw, reed, or similar materials fastened together to shed water and sometimes to provide thermal insulation.

Roof curb
A pitched roof that slopes away from the ridge in two successive planes, as a gambrel or mansard roof.

Roof drain
A drain designed to receive water collecting on the surface of a roof and to discharge it into a leader or a downspout.

Roof gutter
A channel of metal or wood at the eaves or on the roof of a building for carrying off rainwater.

Roof pitch
The slope of a roof usually expressed as a ratio of vertical rise to horizontal run, or in inches of rise per foot of run.

Roof plate
A wall plate which receives the lower ends of roof rafters.

Roof rake
A slope or inclination; the incline from the horizontal of a roof slope.

Roof ridge
The horizontal line at the junction of the upper edge of two sloping roof surfaces.

Roof ridge beam
A beam at the upper ends of the rafters, at the ridge of the roof.

Roof ridgecap
Any covering such as metal, wood, shingles, or tile used to cover the top course of materials at the ridge of a roof.

Roof ridge crest
The ornamentation of the roof ridge.

Roof ridge crest

Roof ridgeroll
A wood strip, rounded on top, which is used to finish the ridges of a roof; often covered with lead sheeting; a metal, tile, or asbestos-cement covering which caps the ridge of a roof.

Roof scupper
An opening in a wall or parapet that allows water to drain from a roof.

Rosette
A round pattern with a carved conventionalized floral motif; a circular decorative wood plaque used in joinery, such as one applied to a wall to receive the end of a stair rail.

Rose window See **Window**.

Rotated
Refers to forms created by revolving a shape on an axis and duplicating it in another location with the same relationship to the central point; as the forms are rotated they are transformed in some manner.

Rotunda
A building that is round both inside and outside, usually covered with a dome.

Rotunda

Round arch See **Arch.**

Round pediment See **Pediment.**

Rounded
Refers to forms that may be spherical, globular, shaped like a ball, or circular in cross section.

Roundel
A small circular panel or window; in glazing, a bulls-eye or circular light like the bottom of a bottle.

Roundel window · See **Window.**

Rover molding See **Molding.**

Row house
One of an unbroken line of houses sharing one or more side-walls in common with its neighbors, usually consisting of uni-form plans, fenestration and other architectural treatments.

Rowlock
A brick laid on its edge so that its end face is visible; one ring of a rowlock arch.

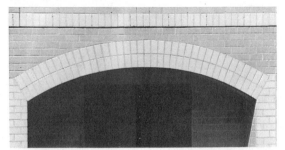

Rubble
Rough stones of irregular shapes and sizes, used in rough, uncoursed work in the construction of walls, foundations, and pavings.

Rubble wall
A rubble wall, either coursed or uncoursed.

Rubblework
Stone masonry built of rubble.

Running bond See Bond.

Running ornament
Any ornamental molding in which the design is continuous in intertwined or flowing lines, as in the representation of foliage and meanders.

Russo-Byzantine architecture
The first phase of Russian architecture (1000–1500) derived from the Byzantine architecture of Greece; it consisted mainly of stone churches characterized by cruciform plans and multiple bulbous domes.

Rust
A substance, usually in powder form, accumulating on the face of steel or iron as a result of oxidation; ultimately weakens or destroys the steel or iron on which it forms.

Rustic
Descriptive of rough, hand-dressed building stone, intentionally laid with high relief, that was frequently used in modest rural structures.

Rustic arch See Arch.

Rusticated masonry See Masonry.

Rustication
Masonry cut in large blocks with the surface left unfinished, separated by deep recessed joints. The border of each block may be beveled or rabbeted on all sides, or top and bottom.

Rustication

Rustic brick See Brick.

Rustic mortar joint See Joint.

Rustic stone masonry See Masonry.

Rustic slate
One of a number of slate shingles of varying thicknesses, yielding an irregular surface when installed.

Rustic stone
Any rough broken stone suitable for rustic masonry, most commonly limestone or sandstone, usually set with the longest dimension exposed horizontally.

Rustic woodwork
Decorative or structural work constructed of unpeeled logs or poles.

Rustic Work
In ashlar masonry, grooved or channeled joints in the horizontal direction, to render them more conspicuous.

S·s

Sailor course bond See **Bond**.

Sakha
In the architecture of India, a door jamb or door frame.

Salient
Any part or prominent
member projecting beyond
a surface.

Saltbox
A wood-framed house, common to colonial new England, which has a short roof pitch in front and a long roof pitch sweeping close to the ground in the back.

Sanctuary
In a church, the immediate area around the principal altar.

Sandstone See **Stone**.

Sarcophagus
An elaborate coffin for an important person, of terra-cotta, wood, stone, metal or other material, decorated with painting, carving, and large enough to contain only the body. If larger, it becomes a tomb.

Sash, window sash
Any framework of a window; may be movable or fixed, may slide in a vertical plane, or may be pivoted.

Sassanian architecture
This architecture (200–600) was prevalent in Persia, primarily in palace complexes. It featured extensive barrel vaults and parabolic domes set on squinches and stuccoed with plaster mortar. The massive walls were covered by pilasters and cornices. The most notable example is the Palace at Ctesiphon.

Satinwood See **Wood**.

Saucer dome See **Dome**.

Sawtooth roof See **Roof**.

Scaffold
A temporary platform to support workers and materials on the face of a structure and to provide access to work areas above the ground; any elaborated platform.

Scaffold

Scagliola See **Plaster**.

Scale
The relationship of one part of an object to an outside measure, such as a human body or some standard reference; a system of representing or reproducing objects in a different size proportionately in every part.

human scale
The size or proportion of a building element or space, or article of furniture, relative to the structural or functional dimensions of the human body.

monumental scale
Impressively large, sturdy
and enduring.

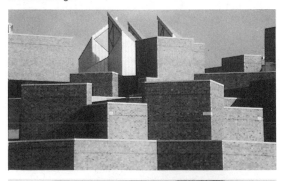

Scallop
One of a continuous series
of curves resembling seg-
ments of a circle, used as a
decorative element on the
outer edge of a strip of
wood used as a molding.

Scalloped capital See **Capital**.

Scarp
A steep slope constructed as a defensive measure in a fortification.

Schematic design phase
The first phase of the architects basic services. The architect
prepares schematic design studies, consisting of drawings illustrating the scale and relationship of the projected components for approval by the owner.

Scheme See **Design**.

Scissors truss See **Truss**.

Sconce
An electric lamp, designed and fabricated for mounting on
a wall, resembling a candlestick or a group of candlesticks.

Scotia molding See **Molding**.

Screen
Any construction whose essential function is merely to separate, protect, seclude, or conceal, but not to support.

Screen facade
A nonstructural facing
assembly used to disguise
the form or overall size of a
building.

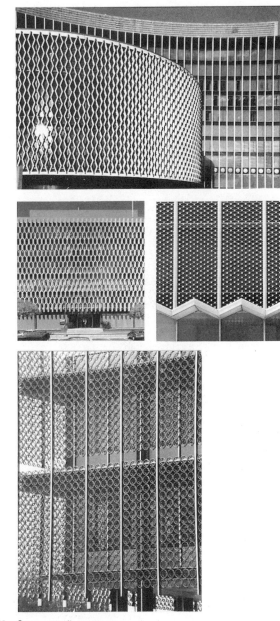

Screen wall See **Wall**.

Scribbled ornament
A decorative effect produced by irregularly distributing lines and scrolls over a surface or on a panel.

Scroll molding   See Molding.

Scroll ornament   See Ornament.

Scrollwork
Ornamental work of any kind in which scrolls, or lines of scroll-like character, are an element.

Sculpture
The art or practice of shaping figures or designs in the round or in relief by carving wood, chiseling marble, modeling clay or casting in metal; any work of art that is created in this manner.

Sculpture

Section
The representation of a building or portion thereof, cut vertically at some imagined plane, so as to show the interior of the space or the profile of the member.

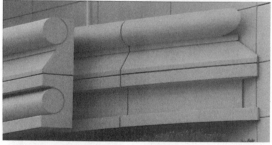

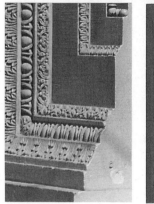

Segmental arch   See **Arch.**

Segmental pediment   See **Pediment.**

Seljuk architecture
An early phase of Turkish Muslim architecture (1000–1200), influenced by Persian architecture, consisting mainly of mosques and minarets.

Semi-arch   See **Arch.**

Semicircular
Describing a form that exhibits an arrangement of objects in the shape of a half-circle, as divided by its diameter.

Semicircular

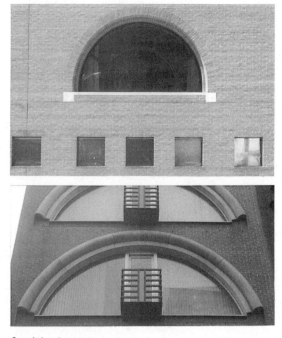

Semicircular arch   See **Arch.**

Semicircular dome   See **Dome.**

Semidome   See **Dome.**

Seminary
A school, academy, college, or university, especially a school for the education of men for the priesthood.

Serpentine
A form that resembles a serpent, showing a sinuous winding movement; a greenish brown or spotted mineral used as a decorative stone used in architectural work.

Serrated
Consisting of notches on the edges, like a saw.

Setback
The upper section of a building, successively recessed, produces a ziggurat effect, admitting light and air to the streets below.

193

Sgraffito

Decoration produced by covering a surface, such as plaster or enamel, of one color with a thin coat of a similar material of another color and scratching through the outer coat to show the color beneath.

Shaft

The main body of a column, pilaster or pier between the capital and the base, or a thin vertical member attached to a wall or pier, often supporting an arch or vaulting rib.

Shafting

In medieval architecture, an arrangement of shafts, combined in the mass of a pier or jamb, so that corresponding groupings of archivolt moldings above may start from their caps at the impost line.

Shafting

Shake See **Wood products.**

Shape

Implies a three-dimensional definition that indicates outline and bulk of the outlined area.

Sheathing

The wood covering placed over the exterior studding or rafters of a building, to provide a base for the application of wall or roof cladding.

Shed

A rough structure for shelter, storage or a workshop; it may be a separate building or a lean-to against another structure, often with one or more open sides.

Shed dormer See **Dormer.**

Shed dormer window See **Window.**

Shed roof See **Roof.**

Sheet glass See **Glass.**

Sheet metal

A flat, rolled metal product, rectangular in cross section and formed with sheared, slit, or sawn edges.

Sheetrock

A proprietary name for gypsum wallboard.

Shell ornament

Any decoration where a shell form is a characteristic part; coquillage.

Shell ornament

Shells
Hollow structures in the form of thin curved slabs, plates or membranes that are self- supporting they are called form-resistant structures because they are shaped according to the loads they carry.

Shikkui   See **Plaster.**

Shiner course bond   See **Bond.**

Shingle   See **Wood products.**

Shingle style
A style (1880–1895) which featured an eclectic American adaptation of New England forms to the structuralism of the Victorian era. Structures were deemphasized by a uniform covering of entire surfaces of the roof and walls with monochromatic shingles; the eaves of the roofs are close to the walls to emphasize the homogeneous shingle covering. The houses in this style were rambling and horizontal and featured wide verandas and hipped roofs.

Shiplap siding   See **Wood products.**

Shoe
A piece of timber, stone, or metal, shaped to receive the lower end of any member, also called a soleplate; a metal base plate for an arch or truss shaped to resist the lateral thrust.

Shoji
A very lightweight sliding partition used in Japanese architecture, consisting of a wooden lattice covered on one side with translucent white rice paper. The lattice is most often composed of small horizontal rectangles.

Shoro
A small structure from which a bell is hung in a Japanese temple compound.

Shoulder
A projection or break changing the thickness or width of a piece of shaped wood, metal, or stone.

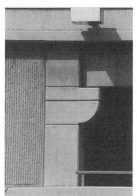

Shouldered arch   See **Arch.**

Siamese (Thai) architecture
An architecture (1350–1500) consisting of stupas and temples. The most characteristic forms are the eaves of overlapping roof planes, which are terminated with sculptural finials. The Temple of the Emerald Buddha in Bangkok is the most notable example.

Sidewalk bridge   See **Bridge**

Sill

The horizontal exterior member at the bottom of a window or door opening, usually sloped away from the bottom of the window or door for drainage of water, and overhanging the wall below.

Sillcourse

In stone masonry, a stringcourse set at the windowsill level, commonly differentiated from the wall by its greater projection, finish, or thickness.

Similarity

The state or quality of being alike in substance, essentials, or characteristics.

Simulated architecture

An architecture that would consist of holographic images of forms and monuments projected into space by laser beams.

Siras

In Indian architecture, the capital of a column or pillar.

Site

An area or plot of ground with defined limits on which a building, project, or part is located or proposed to be located; the specific location of a building or buildings.

Site plan

A plan of a construction site showing the dimensions and contours of the lot and the dimensions of the building or portion thereof to be erected.

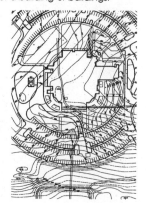

Site relationship

The plot of land where something was, is, or will be located; the situation or position of a place, town, or building, especially with reference to the surrounding locality.

Skeletal frame

Refers to a structural framework of members, originally concealed within a building, or as a self-supporting grid of timber, steel, or concrete.

Skewback

The sloping surface of a member which receives the component materials of an arch.

Skewed

Having an oblique position, or twisted to one side.

Skintled bond See Bond.

Skirt roof See Roof.

Skylight

An opening in a roof which is glazed with a transparent or translucent material used to admit natural or diffused light to the space below.

Skyscraper

Skyscraper

A building of extreme height containing many stories, constructed of a steel or concrete frame which supports the exterior walls, as opposed to a load-bearing structure.

Skywalk   See **Bridge**

Slab

The upper part of a reinforced concrete floor, which is carried on beams below; a concrete mat poured on subgrade, serving as a floor rather than as a structural member.

Slate   See **Stone**.

Sleeper

A horizontal timber laid on a slab or on the ground and to which the subflooring is nailed; any long horizontal beam, at or near the ground, which distributes the load from the posts to the foundation.

Sliding door   See **Door**.

Sliding sash window   See **Window**.

Socle

A low, plain base course for a pedestal, column, or wall; a plain plinth.

Soffit

A ceiling or exposed underside surface of entablatures, archways, balconies, beams, lintels or columns.

Soffit

Solar collector
A device designed to absorb radiation from the sun and transfer this energy to air or a fluid passing through a collector.

Solar heating, active
A solar heating system using mechanical means, such as solar collectors, fans, or pumps, to collect, store, and distribute solar energy.

Solar heating, passive
A solar heating system using a building's site orientation, design, and construction to collect, store, and distribute heat with a minimal use of fans or pumps, relying on the natural flow of heat.

Solar heating system
An assembly of subsystems and components which converts solar energy into thermal energy and uses it for heating.

Solar house
A building so designed that the sun's rays are used to maximum advantage in heating, supplementing or replacing other heating methods.

Solar orientation
The placing of a building in relation to the sun to maximize the amount of heat gained during the coldest months and minimize the amount of heat gained during the warmest months.

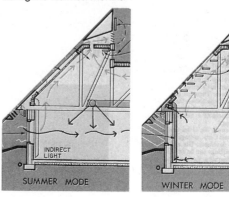

Solarium
In ancient architecture, a terrace on top of a flat-roofed house or over a porch, surrounded by a parapet wall but open to the sky; a sunny room with more glass than usual, and often used for therapy.

Soldier course bond See Bond.

Solid-core door See Door.

Sorin
The crowning spire on a Japanese pagoda, usually made of bronze.

Sound
The sensation stimulated in the auditory organs by a vibratory disturbance.

Sound barrier
Any solid obstacle which is relatively opaque to sound that blocks the line of sight between a sound source and the point of reception of the sound.

Sound insulated glass See Glass.

Sound insulation
The use of structures and materials designed to reduce the transmission of sound from one room or area of a building to another, or from the exterior to the interior of the building.

Sound lock
A vestibule or entranceway which has highly absorptive walls, ceiling, and a carpeted floor; used to reduce the transmission of noise into an auditorium, rehearsal room or studio, or from the area outside.

Space

The unlimited continuous three-dimensional expanse in which all material objects exist; all the area in and around a structure, or volume between specified boundaries, and the interval between two objects.

Space frame

A three-dimensional structural framework made up of interconnected triangular elements that enclose a space, as opposed to a frame where all the elements lie in a single plane.

Spall

A small fragment or chip dislodged from the face of a stone or masonry unit by a blow or by the action caused by the elements, such as a freezing and thawing cycle.

Span

The interval between any two consecutive supports of a beam, girder, or truss or between the opening of an arch.

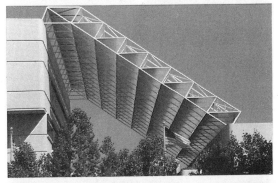

199

199

Spandrel

The triangular space formed between the sides of adjacent arches and the line across their tops; in a skeletal frame building, the walls inside the columns and between the top of the window and the sill above.

Spandrel panel

A panel covering the spandrel area between the head of a window on one level and the sill of the window immediately above.

Spandrel panel

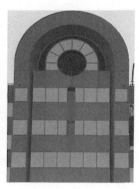

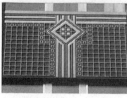

spandrel wall

A wall built on the extrados of an arch, filling the spandrels.

Spanish Colonial Revival style

A unique feature of this revival style (1915–1940) is the ornate low-relief carvings highlighting arches, columns, window surrounds, cornices and parapets. Red-tiled hipped roofs and arcaded porches are typical. Exterior walls are left exposed or finished in plaster or stucco. Iron window grilles and balconies are prevalent. A molded or arcaded cornice highlights the eaves, and large buildings have ornamental parapets and a symbolic bell tower.

Spanish Colonial style

Adobe-brick wall construction covered with a lime wash or plaster characterized this style (1650–1840). Rounded roof beams were extended over porches, which were covered with tile roofs. Missions of the southwestern United States were richly ornamented vernacular interpretations of this Baroque-like style.

Spanish tile See Tile.

Specifications
A part of the contract documents, consisting of written descriptions of a technical nature; of materials, equipment, construction systems, building standards, and workmanship.

Spherical
Refers to a three-dimensional surface, all parts of which are equidistant from a fixed point.

Sphinx See animal forms.

Spiral
Refers to forms that are generated by a continuous curve, traced by a point moving around a fixed point in a fixed plane, while steadily increasing the distance from that point.

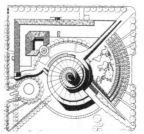

Spiral stair See Stair.

Spire
A tall tapering structure surmounted a steeple or tower.

Splay
A sloped surface which makes an oblique angle with another at the sides of a door or window, with the opening larger on one side than the other; a large chamfer; a reveal at an oblique angle.

Splayed arch See Arch.

Splayed jamb
Any jamb whose face is not at right angles to the wall in which it is set.

Splayed mullion
A mullion that joins two glazed units which are at an angle to each other, such as the mullion of a bay window.

Splayed window
A window whose frame is set at an angle with respect to the face of the wall.

Splice
To connect, unite, or join two similar members, wires, columns or pieces; usually in a straight line, by fastening the lapped ends by means of mechanical end connectors, or by welding.

butt splice
A butt joint, which is further secured by nailing a piece of wood to each side of a butt joint.

lap splice
A splice made by placing one piece on top of another and fastening them together with pins, nails, screws, bolts, rivets, or similar devices.

Spline joint . See Joint.

Spout
A short channel or tube used to spill storm water from gullies, balconies, exterior galleries, so that the water will fall clear of the building; a gargoyle.

Sprayed fireproof insulation
A mixture of mineral fiber with other ingredients, such as asbestos, applied by air pressure with a spray gun; used to provide fire protection or thermal insulation.

Springer
The impost or place where the vertical support for an arch terminates and the curve of the arch begins; the lower voussoir, or bottom stone of an arch, which lies immediately on an impost.

Springing
The point at which an arch rises from its supports.

Springing line
The imaginary horizontal line at which an arch or vault begins to curve; the line in which the springers rest on the imposts.

Sprinkler system
A system, usually automatic, for protection against fire; when activated, it sprays water over a large area in a systematic pattern.

Spur
A decorative appendage on the corners of the base of a round column resting on a square or polygonal plinth, in the form of a grotesque, a tongue, or leafwork.

Square
A regular four-sided figure with equal sides and four equal right angles; may be subdivided along the diagonals or oblique lines connecting the corner angles and the lines connecting the center of each side.

Square

Square billet molding See Molding.

Square rubble masonry See Masonry.

Square-headed
Cut off at right angles, as
an opening with upright
parallel sides and a straight
horizontal lintel, as distinguished from an arched
opening.

Squinch
Corbeling built at the upper corners of a structural bay to
support a smaller dome or drum; a small arch across the
corner of a square room which supports a superimposed octagonal structure above.

Squinch arch See Arch.

Stack bond See Bond.

Stadium
A sports arena, usually oval
or horseshoe-shaped.

Staff
Ornamental plastering, made in molds and reinforced with
fiber, usually nailed or wired into place.

Stained glass See Glass.

Stained glass window See Window.

Stainless steel See Metal.

Stair
A series of steps or flights of
steps for traveling between
two or more successive
levels with connecting
landings at each level,
either on the exterior or in
the interior.

box stair
An interior staircase constructed with a closed string on both sides, often enclosed by walls or partitions with door openings at various floor levels.

circular stair
A stair having a cylindrical shape.

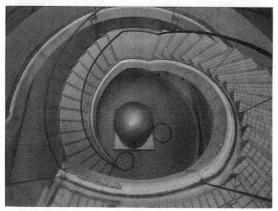

flight
A continuous series of steps with no intermediate landings.

open stair
A stair or stairway, whose treads are visible on one or both sides and open to a room in which it is located.

spiral stair
A flight of stairs, circular in plan, whose treads wind around a central newel, or post.

winding stair
Any stair constructed chiefly or entirely of winders.

Staircase
A vertical element of access in a structure for ascending or descending from one level to another. The form of the staircase is often expressed on the exterior of the building if it is located adjacent to an exterior wall.

Stair tower
A part of a structure containing a winding stair filling it exactly; a stair enclosure which projects beyond the roof of a building.

Standing seam joint See Joint.

Station point see Perspective projection

Statue
A form of likeness sculpted, modeled, carved, or cast in material such as stone, clay, wood, or bronze.

Stave church
A Scandinavian church of the 12th and 13th centuries constructed entirely of wood with few windows and a steep roof; highly original in structure with fantastic semipagan decorative features.

Steamboat Gothic style
A richly ornamental mode of Gothic Revival building (1850–1880) in the Ohio and Mississippi River Valleys, characterized by the gingerbread ornamental construction found on riverboats of the Victorian period.

Steel See Metal.

Steel frame
A skeleton of steel beams and columns providing all that is structurally necessary for the building to stand.

Steeple

A tall ornamental structure terminating in a spire and surmounting the tower of a church or public building.

Stele

An upright stone slab or pillar with a carved or inscribed surface, used as a monument or marker, or as a commemorative tablet in the face of a building.

Step

A stair unit which consists of one tread, the horizontal upper surface, and one riser, the vertical face.

bull-nosed step

A step usually the lowest in a flight, having one or both ends rounded to a semicircle and projecting beyond the face of the stair string. The projection extends beyond and around the newel post.

cantilever step

Steps built into the wall at one end, but supported at the other end only by the steps below.

curtail step

A step, usually lowest in a flight, of which one or both ends are rounded into a spiral or scroll shape which projects beyond the newel.

riser

The vertical face of a stair step.

tread

The horizontal upper surface of a step; includes the rounded edge or nosing which extends over the riser.

Stepped

Refers to forms that are increased or decreased by a series of successive increments or modulated by incremental stages or steps.

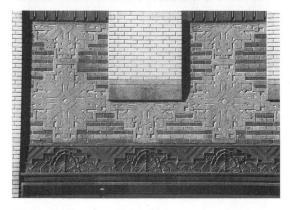

Stepped arch See **Arch.**

Stepped gable See **Gable.**

Stepped pyramid

An early type of pyramid having a stepped and terraced appearance.

Stereobate

The substructure, foundation, or solid platform upon which a building is erected. In a columnar building, it includes the uppermost step or platform upon which the columns stand.

Stile

One of the upright structural members of a frame, such as at the outer edge of a door or a window sash.

Stone

Native rock that has been processed by shaping, cutting or sizing for building or landscaping use. It is fire-resistant and varies according to type, from fairly porous to impregnable. There are three basic types of stone: igneous, such as granite, is long lasting and durable; sedimentary, such as limestone, is made up of organic remains; metamorphic rock is either igneous or sedimentary transformed by pressure and heat or both.

alabaster

A fine-grained, translucent variety of very pure gypsum, white or delicately shaded, and used for ornamental work.

bluestone

A dense, fine-grained sandstone that splits easily along bedding planes to form thin slabs.

brownstone

A dark brown or reddish-brown sandstone, used extensively for building in the United States during the middle and late nineteenth century.

dolomite

Limestone consisting principally of the mineral dolomite.

fieldstone

Loose stone found on the surface or in the soil, flat in the direction of bedding and suitable for use as dry wall masonry.

gneiss

A coarse-grained, dark metamorphic rock; composed mainly of quartz, feldspar, mica, and other minerals corresponding in composition to granite, in which the minerals are arranged in layers.

granite

An igneous rock having crystals or grains of visible size; consists mainly of quartz, and mica or other colored minerals.

limestone

Rock of sedimentary origin composed principally of calcite, dolomite or both; used as a building stone or crushed-stone aggregate, or burnt to produce lime.

marble

Metamorphic rock made up largely of calcite or dolomite; capable of taking a high polish, and used especially in architecture and sculpture; numerous minerals account for the distinctive appearance.

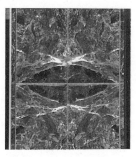

obsidian
A natural volcanic glass, usually black with a bright luster, and transparent in thin slabs.

quartzite sandstone
A variety of sandstone composed largely of granular quartz cemented by silica, forming a homogeneous mass of very high tensile and crushing strengths; used as a building stone, and as an aggregate in concrete.

sandstone
Sedimentary rock that is composed of sand-sized grains, naturally cemented by mineral materials.

serpentine
A group of minerals consisting of hydrous magnesium silicate, or rock largely composed of these minerals; commonly occurs in greenish shades; used as decorative stone.

slate
A hard, brittle metamorphic rock characterized by good cleavage along parallel planes; used as cut stone in thin sheets for flooring, roofing, panels, and in granular form as surfacing on composition roofing.

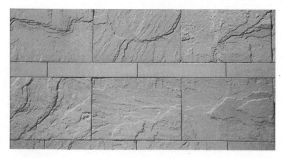

travertine
A variety of limestone deposited by springs, usually banded, commonly coarse and cellular, often containing fossils; used as building stones, especially for interior facing or flooring.

verde antique
A dark green serpentine rock marked with white veins of calcite which takes a high polish; used for decorative purposes since ancient times; sometimes classified as a marble.

volcanic stone
A low-density, high-porosity rock composed of volcanic particles, ranging from ash size to small pebble size, which are compacted or cemented together; used as a building stone or as a thermal insulation material.

Stone Age
The earliest known period of human culture, characterized by the use of stone tools and weapons.

Stool
The flat piece upon which a window closes, corresponding to the sill of a door.

Stoop
A platform or small porch at the entrance to a house, usually up several steps.

Stop
The molding or trim on the inside face of a door or window frame against which the door or window closes.

Story
The space in a building between floor levels; in some codes a basement is considered a story, generally a cellar is not; a major architectural division even where no floor exists, as a tier or a row of windows.

Streetscape
A diminutive version of the cityscape, relating elements on the ground plane to the viewer; some of the elements consist of building setbacks, trees, parks and open areas, street furniture and signage.

Stressed skin panel   See **Wood products.**

Stretcher
A masonry unit laid horizontally with its length in the direction of the face of the wall.

String
In a stair, an inclined board which supports the end of the steps; also called a stringer.

face string
An outer string, usually of better material or finish than the rough string which it covers; may be part of the actual construction or applied to the face of the supporting member.

outer string
The string at the outer and exposed edge of a stair, away from the wall.

Stringcourse
A horizontal band of masonry, extending across the facade to mark a division in a wall, often encircling decorative features such as pillars or engaged columns; may be flush or projecting, molded or richly carved.

Struck molding   See **Molding.**

Struck mortar joint   See **Mortar joint.**

Structural engineering
A branch of engineering concerned with the design and construction of structures to withstand physical forces or displacements without danger of collapse or without loss of serviceability or function.

Structural glass   See **Glass.**

Structural shape
A hot-rolled steel beam of standardized cross section, temper, size, and alloy; includes angle iron, channels, tees, I-beams, and H sections, and is commonly used for structural purposes.

Strut

A bracing member, or any piece of a frame which resists thrusts in the direction of its own length, whether upright, horizontal or diagonal.

Stuart style

A style (1603–1688) typifying the late English Renaissance.

Stucco

An exterior fine plaster finish composed of portland cement, lime, and sand mixed with water, used for decorative work or moldings, and usually textured.

Stud

One of a series of upright posts or vertical structural members which act as the supporting elements in a wall or partition.

Study   See **Design.**

Stupa

A Buddhist memorial site, consisting of an artificial mound on a platform, surrounded by an outer ambulatory with four gateways, and crowned by a multiple sunshade, erected to enshrine a relic.

Stylobate

The single top course of the three steps forming a foundation of a classical temple upon which the columns rests; any continuous base, plinth, or pedestal upon which a row of columns rests directly.

Subdivision

A tract of land divided into residential lots.

Suborder

A secondary architectural order, introduced chiefly for decoration, as distinguished from a main order of a structure.

Sullivanesque style

A style (1890–1920) named for Louis Henry Sullivan, noted for his stylized ornamentation and simple multistory forms, designed as if they were classical columns; uninterrupted to express height, much the same as fluting. Vertical rows of windows were separated by ornamented panels; the massive decorative cornice resembled the capital. An intricate weaving of linear forms with stylized foliage was highlighted with low-relief ornamentation in terra-cotta.

Sullivanesque style

Sumerian architecture
An architecture (5000–2000 B.C.) made of locally available materials: clay tied bundles of reeds used as structural framing for huts and halls, with sun-dried bricks for the walls between these buttresses. Monumental temples and palaces were built around a series of courtyards; the ziggurat of Ur is the most famous. Large cities had well-developed drainage and sewer systems, and were protected by strong ramparts.

Sun deck
A roof area, balcony, or open porch which is exposed to the sun.

Sun disk
A disk representing the sun with wings, especially used in Egyptian antiquity as emblematic of the sun god.

Sunk draft
A margin around a building stone which is sunk below the face of the stone to give it a raised appearance.

Sunk molding   See Molding.

Sunk panel
A panel recessed below the surface of its surrounding framing or carved into solid masonry or timber.

Supercolumniation
The placing of one order of columns above another in a classical structure, usually with the most ornate orders at the top.

Supermarket
A large, self-service, retail market which sells food, household goods, and household merchandise.

Surbased arch   See Arch.

Surround
An encircling border or decorative frame around a door, window or other opening.

Survey
A boundary or topographic mapping of a site; a compilation of the measurements of an existing building; an analysis of a building for use of the interior space.

Suspended ceiling   See Ceiling

Suspended forms
Refers to forms that are hung so as to allow free movement, and appear to be supported without attachment to any objects below.

Suspended roof   See Roof

Swag
A festoon, hung between rosettes or other terminals.

Symbol

THE EMPLOYERS' LIABILITY
ASSURANCE CORPORATION, LIMITED

Symbol
Something that stands for or represents something else by association, resemblance, or convention, deriving its meaning chiefly from the structure on which it appears.

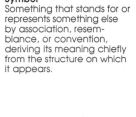

Symmetry
The exact correspondence of forms of similar size and arrangement of parts, equidistant and on opposite sides of a dividing line or plane about the center line or axis.

bilateral symmetry
A balanced arrangement of identical similar elements about a central axis.

Systems Design
Three definitions characterize this approach to problem solving. The first is the design of a range of components to be prefabricated in factories and combined in different ways to yield different types of structures. The second is the application of analysis to the supply of materials and assembly processes. The third is a conceptual overview of design where each building is regarded as part of a greater whole and each project is seen in its social, cultural and economic context.

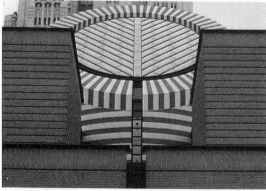

radial symmetry
Balanced elements that radiate from a central point.

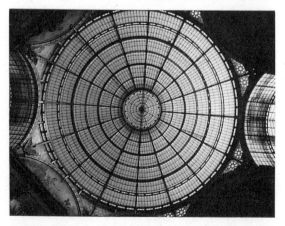

Synagogue
A place of assembly or a building for Jewish worship and religious instruction.

T·t

Table
Applied generally to all horizontal bands of moldings, base moldings and cornices.

Tablero
A rectangular framed panel which is cantilevered over an outward sloping apron, with which it is always used; characteristic of the temples at Teotihuacan in Mexico.

Tablet
A rectangularly shaped separate panel or flat slab, often bearing an inscription or carving of an image.

Talud
In Mesoamerican architecture, an outer wall or facade which slopes inward as a structure's height increases. The feature first appeared at the Olmec site of La Venta, Tabasco Mexico around 800 BC.

Talud-tablero
A feature combining a tablero with a sloping talud, over which it is cantilevered. This combination is repeated over the facade of stepped pyramids, an original contribution of Teotihuacan architecture.

Tapering
Forms exhibiting a gradual diminution in thickness, or reduction in cross section, as in a spire or column.

Tatami
A thick straw floor mat in a Japanese house covered with finely woven reeds and bound with plain or decorated bands of silk, cotton, or hemp; its size of 3 feet by 6 feet is used as a standard unit of measurement.

Teahouse
A Japanese garden house used for the tea ceremony.

Teak   See Wood.

Tee
A finial in the form of a conventionalized umbrella; in Japanese architecture on stupas and pagodas.

Tepee
A tent of the American Indians, made usually from animal skins laid on a conical frame of long poles and having an opening at the top for ventilation and a flap door.

Tempera
A rapidly drying paint consisting of egg white, gum, pigment, and water, used in painting murals.

Tempered glass   See Glass.

Template
A pattern of sheet material, used as a guide for setting out work and in repeating patterns of painted ornamentation.

Temple
An edifice dedicated to the service of a deity or deities and connected with a system of worship; an edifice erected as a place of public worship, especially a Protestant church.

Tendril
A long, slender, coiling extension, such as a stem, serving as an ornamental device; used primarily by Art Nouveau architects.

Tensile structure

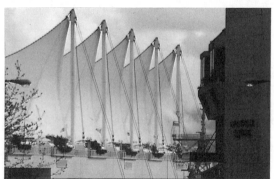

Tenon
The projecting end of a piece of wood or other material, reduced in cross section so that it may be inserted into a corresponding mortise in another piece to form a secure joint.

Tensile structures
Those that stretch or extend a member or other ductile material such as a fabric or or membrane; some forms express this quality even if the material is not fabric, such as concrete shells.

Tension column See Column.

Terminal
A terminus occurring at the end of a series of incidents, as a resting point; a point of emphasis, as in an object situated at the end of an element.

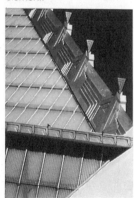

Termination

An ornamental element which finishes off an architectural feature.

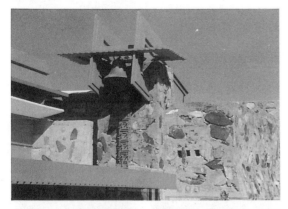

Terminus

A bust or figure of the upper part of the human body terminated in a plain rectangular block, sometimes attached to a wall as a pillar or springing out of a column.

Terrace
A flat roof or raised space or platform adjoining a building, paved or planted, especially one used for leisure enjoyment.

Terra-cotta
A hard-burnt glazed or unglazed clay unit, plain or ornamental, machine-extruded or hand-molded, usually larger in size than brick or facing tile, used in building construction.

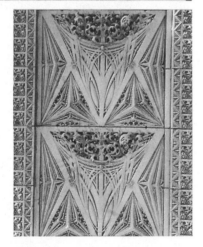

Terrazzo
Marble-aggregate concrete that is cast in place or precast and ground smooth, used as a decorative surface for walls and floors.

Tesselated
Formed of small square pieces of marble, stone, or glass in the manner of an ornamental mosaic.

Tessera
A small square piece of colored marble, glass, or tile, used to make geometric or figurative mosaic patterns.

Tetrahedron
A polygon with four plane surfaces.

Texture
The tactile and visual quality of a surface as distinct from its color or form, as showing a grainy, coarse, tactile or dimensional quality as opposed to a uniformly flat, smooth aspect.

Thatch
A roof covering made of straw, reed, or similar materials fastened together to shed water and sometimes to provide thermal insulation; in tropical countries palm leaves are widely used.

Thatched roof   See Roof.

Theater
A building or outdoor structure providing a stage and associated equipment for the presentation of dramatic or musical performances and seating for spectators.

Theme
An idea, point of view, or perception embodied in a work of art; an underlying and essential subject of artistic expression.

theme variation
Repetition of a theme with embellishments in rhythm, details and materials while keeping the essential characteristics of the original.

theme development
To disclose by degree or in detail, to evolve the possibilities by a process of growth; to elaborate with the gradual unfolding of an idea.

Thermal barrier
An element of low heat conductivity placed on an assembly to reduce or prevent the flow of heat between highly conductive materials; used in metal window or curtain wall designs in cold climates.

Thermal conduction
The process of heat transfer through a material medium, in which kinetic energy is transmitted by particles of the material without displacement of the particles.

Thermal expansion
The change in length or volume which a material or body undergoes on being heated.

Three-centered arch See **Arch.**

Three-hinged arch See **Arch.**

Three-point perspective see **Perspective projection**

Threshold
A strip fastened to the floor beneath a door, to cover the joint where two types of floor materials meet or to provide weather protection.

Throat
A groove which is cut along the underside of a member, as a stringcourse or coping on a wall, to prevent water from running back towards the wall.

Tie beam See **Beam.**

Tie rod
A rod in tension, used to hold parts of a structure together.

Tile
A ceramic surfacing unit, usually thin in relation to the facial area; made from clay or a mixture of clay and other ceramic materials; has either a glazed or an unglazed face.

ceramic mosaic tile
An unglazed tile, usually mounted on sheets to facilitate setting, may be either composed of porcelain or natural clay.

clay tile
A roofing tile of hard, burnt clay. In flooring it is called a quarry tile.

crest tile
Tile which fits like a saddle on the ridge of a roof.

encaustic tile

A tile for pavement and wall decoration, in which the pattern is inlaid or incrusted in clay of one color in a ground of clay of another color.

glazed tile

Ceramic tile having a fused impervious glazed surface finish, composed of ceramic materials fused into the body of the tile; the body may be nonvitreous, semivitreous, or impervious.

mission tile

A clay roofing tile, approximately semicylindrical in shape; laid in courses with the units having their convex side alternately up and down.

paving tile

Unglazed porcelain or natural clay tile, formed by the dust-pressed method; similar to ceramic mosaic tile in composition and physical properties, but thicker.

ridge tile

A tile which is curved in section, often decorative, used to cover the ridge of a roof.

unglazed tile

A hard, dense ceramic tile for floor or walls; of homogeneous composition, and deriving its color and texture from the materials and the method of manufacture.

vinyl-asbestos tile

A resilient, semiflexible floor tile; composed of asbestos fibers, limestone, plasticizers, pigments, and a polyvinyl chloride resin binder; has good wearing qualities, high grease resistance, and relatively good resilience.

Tilt-up construction

Construction of concrete wall panels which are cast horizontally, adjacent to their final positions, and then tilted up into a vertical position when hardened.

Timber

Uncut trees that are suitable for construction or conversion to lumber.

Timber-framed building

A building having timbers as its structural elements, except for the foundations.

Tin See **Metal.**

Tinted glass See **Glass.**

Toltec architecture

An austere geometric architecture (750–1200) formed the basis for the Aztec style and others. It was characterized by the use of colonnades, square carved roof supports, monumental serpent columns, and narrative relief panels set in plain wall surfaces. Tula was one of the major sites in this style, which featured colossal statues of warriors and stone panels carved with human-headed jaguars and carved symbols of Quetzalcoatl.

Tomb

In architecture, a memorial structure over or beside a grave.

Tombstone light
A small window with lights in the shape of an arched tomb-stone, usually in the transom above a doorway.

Tongue and groove joint   See **Joint.**

Tooled mortar joint   See **Mortar joint.**

Topiarium opus
A wall painting representing trees, shrubs, and trellis work, as at Pompeii.

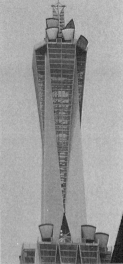

Topiary work
The clipping or trimming of plants, trees, and shrubs, usually evergreens, into or-namental and fantastic shapes.

Torana   See **Gate.**

Torii   See **Gate.**

Torus
A bold projecting molding, convex in profile, forming the lowest member of a base over a plinth or other projection from a wall sur-face.

Torus molding   See **Molding.**

Tou-kung
A cantilevered bracket in traditional Chinese construction; tiers or clusters of brackets are used to carry rafters which support purlins far beyond the outermost columns of a building.

Tower

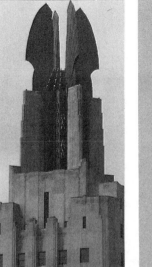

Tower
A tall structure designed for observation, communica-tion or defense. A bell tower is synonymous with the term "campanile"; church towers were used for hanging bells, hence the use of the term "belfry."

Town hall
A public hall or building, belonging to a town, where public offices are established, the town council meets, and the people assemble for town meetings.

Town house
An urban building without sideyards, containing one residence on one or more floors.

Townscape
A view of a town or city from a single vantage point; the planning and construction of buildings within a town or city with the objective of achieving overall aesthetically pleasing relationships.

Trabeated
Descriptive of construction using beams or lintels, following the principle of post and lintel construction, as distinguished from construction using arches and vaults.

Tracery
The curvilinear ornamental branchlike shapes of stone or wood creating an openwork pattern of mullions, so treated as to be ornamental within the upper part of a Gothic window or opening of similar character.

bar tracery
A pattern formed by interlocking branching mullions within the arch of Gothic window tracery.

blind tracery
Tracery that is not pierced through.

branch tracery
A form of Gothic tracery in Germany made to imitate rustic work with boughs and knots.

fan tracery
Tracery on the soffit of a vault whose ribs radiate like the ribs of a fan.

geometric tracery
Gothic tracery characterized by a pattern of geometric shapes, as circles and foils.

intersecting tracery
Tracery formed by the upward curving, forking and continuation of the mullions, springing from alternate mullions or from every third mullion and intersecting each other.

plate tracery
Tracery whose openings are or seem to be pierced through thin slabs of stone.

perpendicular tracery
Tracery of the Perpendicular style with repeated perpendicular mullions, crossed at intervals by horizontal transoms, producing repeated vertical rectangles which often rise to the full curve of the arch.

reticulated tracery
Gothic tracery consisting mainly of a netlike arrangement of repeated geometrical figures.

Transformation
The metamorphosis that occurs where primary shapes and forms are changed into additive or subtractive forms.

Translucency
The quality of a material that transmits light sufficiently diffused to eliminate any perception of distinct images beyond.

Transom
A horizontal bar of wood or stone across a door or window; the cross-bar separating a door from the fanlight above it; a window divided by a transom bar.

Transom bar
An intermediate horizontal member of a doorframe or window frame; a horizontal member which separates a door from a window, panel or louver above.

Transom light
A glazed light above the transom bar of a door.

Transparency
The quality of a material that is capable of transmitting light so that objects or images may easily be seen on the other side.

Transparency

Transverse arch See Arch

Transverse section see **Projection drawing**

Trapezoid
A four-sided figure with unequal sides; a parallel trapezoid has two unequal parallel sides, and two equal nonparallel sides; a symmetrical trapezoid has two pairs of adjacent equal sides.

Travertine See Stone.

Tread See Step.

Trefoil arch See Arch.

Trellis
A structural frame supporting an open latticework or grating constructed of either metal or wood, used to support plants or vines or left exposed.

221

Tresse
Flat or convex bandelets
which are intertwined;
especially such interlocking
ornamentation used to
adorn buildings.

Tresse molding   See **Molding**.

Triangular arch   See **Arch**.

Triangle
A plane geometrical figure
with three sides and three
angles; the equilateral triangle has both equal sides
and equal angles.

Triangulated
Refers to any construction
based on a continuous
series of triangles for stability; particularly evident in
designs for atrium skylights
and other space frames.

Triangulated

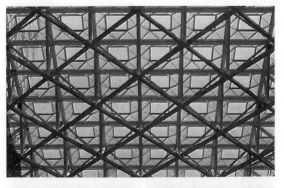

Tribunal
In an ancient Roman basilica, a raised platform for the chair
of the magistrates; a place of honor.

Triglyph
A characteristic ornament
of the Doric frieze, consisting of raised blocks of three
vertical bands separated by
V-shaped grooves, alternating with plain or sculptured
panels called metopes.

Trilith
A monument, or part of a
monument, consisting of
two upright stones sup-
porting a horizontal stone,
as at Stonehenge and other
ancient sires.

222

Trim

The visible woodwork on moldings, such as baseboards, cornices, casings around doors and windows; any visible element, which covers or protects joints, edges, or ends of another material.

Trimetric projection see **Projection drawing**

Trimmer

A piece of timber in a roof, floor, or wooden partition, to support a header which in turn supports the ends of the joists, rafters, or studs; a small horizontal beam, into which the ends of one or more joists are framed.

Triton

A sea monster, half man and half fish, often used in classical and Renaissance ornamentation.

Triumphal arch

An arch commemorating the return of a victorious army, usually located along the line of march during a triumphal procession.

Trompe l'oeil

A phrase meaning "that which deceives the eye", it was originally used to describe precisely rendered views of earlier architectural styles, wherein painters produced a convincing illusion of reality. This has been applied to exterior and interior mural design where architectural elements and entire facades have been painted on blank expanses of buildings, indicating a particular architectural style, period, or design.

Trompe L'oeil

Trophy
A sculptural composition of arms and armor as an emblem of, or a memorial to, victorious battles or triumphant military figures.

Troweled mortar joint See **Mortar joint.**

Truncated
Forms that have been cut off at one end, usually the apex, often with a plane parallel to the base.

Truss
A composite structural system composed of straight members transmitting only axial tension or compression stresses along each member, joined to form a triangular arrangement.

arched truss
A truss with an arched upper chord and a straight bottom chord, with vertical hangers between the two chords.

bowstring truss
A truss with one curved member in the shape of a bow and a straight or cambered member, which ties together the two ends of the bow.

howe truss
A truss having upper and lower horizontal members, between which are vertical and diagonal members; the vertical web members take tension, and the diagonal web members are under compression.

lattice truss
A truss consisting of upper and lower horizontal chords, connected by web members which cross each other, usually stiffened by joining at the intersection of the braces.

scissors truss
A type of truss used to support a pitched roof; the ties cross each other and are connected to the opposite rafters at an intermediate point along their length.

warren truss
A form of truss having parallel upper and lower chords, with connecting members which are inclined, forming a series of approximately equilateral triangles.

Trussed
Facades with decorative forms derived from trusses that support the structure either horizontally or vertically; featuring triangular patterns or diagonal bracing, expressed in exterior materials subtly or boldly.

224

Trussed

Tudor arch   See **Arch.**

Tudor style
The final development of English Perpendicular Gothic architecture (1485–1547), during the reign of Henry VII and Henry VIII,
preceding Elizabethan architecture and characterized by
the use of four-centered arches.

Tulipwood   See **Wood.**

Turret
A diminutive tower, charac-
teristically projecting out on
corbels from a corner of the
structure.

Twisted column   See **Column.**

Two-centered arch   See **Arch.**

Two-hinged arch   See **Arch.**

Two-point perspective   see **Perspective projection**

Tympanum
The triangular space be-
tween the horizontal and
sloping cornices immedi-
ately above the opening of
a doorway or a window, or
the space between the lintel
above a door and the arch
above.

U·u

Unbraced frame
A structural framework in which the resistance to lateral load is provided by the bending resistance of its structural members and their connections.

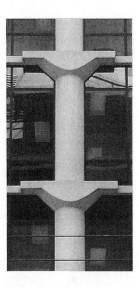

Undercoat
A coat of paint applied on new wood, or over a primer, or over a previous coat of paint; improves the seal and serves as a base for the top coat, for which it provides better adhesion.

Undercut
In stonework, to cut away a lower part, leaving a projection above that serves the function of a drip. To rout a groove or channel back from the edge of an overhanging member.

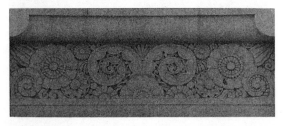

Underpinning
The rebuilding or deepening of the foundation of an existing building to provide additional or improved support, as the result of an excavation in adjoining property that is deeper than the existing foundation.

Undulating
Forms that have a wavelike character or depict sinuous motion with a wavy outline or appearance.

Undulating

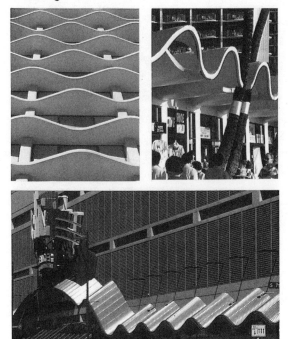

Unglazed tile See **Tile**.

Uniformity
The state or quality of being identical, homogeneous, or regular.

Unity
A oneness and absence of diversity; a combination or arrangement of parts and the ordering of all the elements in a work so that each one contributes to a total single aesthetic effect.

Urban renewal
The improvement of slum, deteriorated, and underutilized area of a city; the rehabilitation of relatively sound structures, and conservation measures to arrest the spread of deterioration.

Urn
A vase of varying size and shape, usually having a footed base or pedestal and used as a decorative device; originally to contain ashes from the dead.

Utopian architecture

A style of architecture (1960–1993), called "fantastic" or "visionary," produced without the constraints of clients, budgets, materials, or building and planning regulations. It is produced in the form of drawings or models that transcend limitations but are unlikely to be constructed, at least in the foreseeable future.

V·v

Valley

The lower trough or gutter formed by the intersection of two inclined planes of a roof.

Valley rafter   See **Rafter**.

Vanishing point   see **Perspective projection**

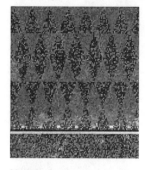

Variegated

Said of a material or surface which is irregularly marked with different colors.

Variety

The state or quality of having varied or diverse forms, types, or characteristics.

Vault

An arched roof or ceiling or a continuous semicircular ceiling that extends in a straight line over a hall, room, or other partially enclosed space.

barrel vault
A masonry vault resting on two parallel walls having the form of a half cylinder; sometimes called a tunnel vault.

conical vault
A vault having a cross section in the form of a circular arc, which is larger at one end than the other.

cross vault
A vault formed by the intersection at right angles of two barrel vaults.

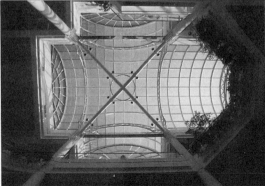

Double vault
A vault, usually domical, consisting of an inner shell separated from a higher outer shell.

fan vault
A concave conical vault whose ribs, of equal length and curvature, radiate from the springing like the ribs of a fan.

rampant vault
A vault, whose two abutments are located on an inclined plane, such as a vault supporting or forming the ceiling of a stairway; the impost on one side is higher than the impost on the other side.

ribbed vault
A vault in which the ribs support, or seem to support, the web of the vault.

Vault capital
The capital of a pier that supports a vault or a rib thereof.

Vaulted
Constructed as a vault.

Vaulting course
A horizontal course made up of abutments or the springers of a vaulted roof.

Vault rib
An arch under the soffit of a vault, appearing to support it.

Vaulting shaft
A colonette in a membered pier that appears to support a rib in a vault.

Veneer
The covering of one material with thin slices of another to give an effect of greater richness.

Venetian arch   See **Arch.**

Venetian door   See **Door.**

Venetian mosaic   See **Mosaic.**

Venetian window   See **Window.**

Ventilator
In a room or building, any device or contrivance used to provide fresh air or expel stale air.

Veranda
Similar to a balcony but located on the ground level; it can extend around one, two or all sides of a building.

Vergeboard
An ornamental board hanging from a projecting roof; a bargeboard.

Vermiculated
Ornamented by regular winding, wandering, and wavy lines, as if caused by the movement of worms.

Vernacular
Native or peculiar to a particular country or locality; a form of building based on regional forms and materials, and concerned with ordinary domestic and functional buildings.

Vertex
The highest point of a structure; the apex or summit.

Vertical pivoting window   See Window.

Vertical sliding window   See Window.

Vestibule
An intermediate chamber or passage located between the entrance and interior or court of a building that serves as a shelter or transitional element from exterior to interior space.

Victorian Gothic style
A colorful style (1860–1890), wherein materials of different colors and textures are juxtaposed, creating decorative bands and highlighting corners, arches and arcades. Materials most often used are ornamental pressed bricks, terra-cotta tile and incised carvings of foliated and geometric patterns. Openings have straight heads as well as pointed Gothic arched heads. In timber frame buildings the gable, porch and eave trim is massive and strong.

Victorian Romanesque style
A polychromatic exterior combined with the semicircular arch highlight this style (1870–1890). Different colored stone or brick for window trim, arches, quoins and belt courses contrasts with the stone wall surface. Decorative bricks and terra-cotta tiles are also used. Round arches are supported by short polished stone columns. Foliated forms, including grotesques and arabesques, decorate the capitals and corbels. Windows vary in size and shape.

Vignette
A portion of a French design for an iron balconet, used as a protection at window openings.

Vihara
A Buddhist or Jain monastery in Indian architecture.

Villa
In Roman and Renaissance periods, a country seat with its dwellings, outbuildings, and gardens, often quite elaborate; in modern times a detached suburban or country house of some pretension.

Vinyl   See Plastic.

Vinyl asbestos tile   See Tile.

Vitruvian scroll

A series of scrolls connected by a stylized wavelike continuous band; also called a wave scroll.

Vitruvian wave molding See Molding.

Volume

The size or extent of any three-dimensional object or region of space; the bulk, size or dimension of a solid body or space.

Volute

A spiral, scroll-like ornament having a twisted or rolled shape, found most often on the capital of the Ionic column.

Vomitory

An entrance or opening, usually one of a series, piercing a bank of seats in a theater or stadium, permitting entry or egress by large numbers of people.

Voussoir

A wedge-shaped block whose converging sides radiate from the center forming an element of an arch or vaulted ceiling.

stepped voussoir

A voussoir which is squared along its upper surfaces so that it fits horizontal courses of masonry units.

W·w

Wainscot
A protective or decorative facing applied to the lower portion of an interior partition or wall, such as wood paneling or other facing material.

Walkway
A passage or lane designated for pedestrian traffic.

Wall
A structure which encloses or subdivides a space with a continuous surface, except where fenestration or other openings occur.

balloon frame wall
A system of framing a wooden building wherein the exterior bearing walls and partitions consists of single studs which extend the full height of the frame from the top of the soleplate to the roof plate.

bearing wall
Supports any vertical load in addition to its own weight.

cant wall
A wall canted in elevation from true vertical.

cavity wall
An exterior wall, usually of masonry, consisting of an outer course and an inner course separated by a continuous air space connected by metal ties.

curtain wall
A method of construction in which all building loads are transmitted to a metal skeleton frame, so that the non-bearing exterior walls of metal and glass are simply a protective cladding.

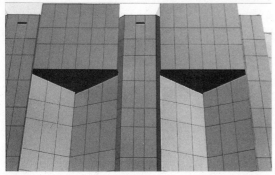

exterior wall
A wall which is part of the envelope of a building, thereby having one face exposed to the weather or to earth.

foundation wall
A wall below or partly below grade to provide support for the exterior walls or other parts of the structure.

half-timbered wall
Descriptive of buildings of the 16th and 17th centuries, which were built with strong timber foundations, supports, knees, and studs, and whose walls were filled in with plaster or masonry materials such as brick.

interior wall
Any wall within a building, entirely surrounded by exterior walls.

load-bearing wall
A wall capable of supporting an imposed load in addition to its own weight.

masonry wall
A bearing or non-bearing wall consisting of hollow masonry units.

non-load-bearing wall
A wall subject only to its own weigh and to wind pressure.

partition
An interior wall dividing a room or part of a building into separate areas, may be either non-load-bearing or bearing.

party wall
A wall used jointly by two parties under an easement agreement, erected upon a line dividing two parcels of land, each one a separate real estate entity; a common wall.

retaining wall
A wall, either freestanding or laterally braced, that bears against earth or other fill surface and resists lateral and other forces from the material in contact with the side of the wall.

screen wall
A movable or fixed device, especially a framed construction, designed to divide, conceal, or protect, but not to support.

screen wall

Wall column See **Column.**

Warehouse
A building designed for the storage of various goods.

Warren truss See **Truss.**

Water table
A horizontal offset in a wall
sloped on the top to throw
off water.

Watertight
An enclosure or barrier that does not permit the passage of moisture.

Wattle and daub
A primitive construction consisting of a coarse basketwork of twigs woven between upright poles, and plastered over with mud.

Wavy
Refers to forms that are arranged into curls or undulations, or any graphic representation of curved shapes, outlines or patterns that resembles such a wave.

weatherboarding
Wood siding commonly used as an exterior covering on a frame building consisting of boards with a rabbeted upper edge that fits under an overlapping board above.

Weathered
Descriptive of a material or surface which has been exposed to the elements for a long period of time; having an upper surface which is splayed so as to allow water to drain off.

Weathered

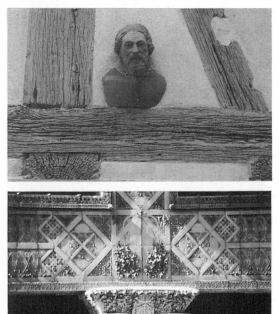

Weathered siding See **Wood products.**

Weathering
An inclination given to the surface of horizontal joints in masonry construction to prevent water from collecting in them.

Weathervane
A metal form, fixed on a rotating spindle that turns to indicates the direction of the wind, usually located on top of a spire, pinnacle or other elevated position on a building.

Weep hole
A small opening in a wall or window member, through which accumulated condensation or water may drain to the building exterior, such as from the base of a cavity wall flashing, or a skylight.

Western Stick style
This adaptation of the Stick style (1890–1920) was characterized by a gently pitched gable roof that extended well beyond the wall and by projecting balconies. A unique feature is the exposed sticklike rafters that project along the roof eaves. Window lintels, railings and other beams extend beyond vertical posts. Pegs were used to join the members, and the ends were rounded off, as were corners of posts and beams. The exterior was finished in wood shingles.

Wheel window   See Window.

White oak   See Wood.

White pine   See Wood.

Wigwam
Eastern native American dwelling, round or oval in plan, with a rounded roof consisting of a bent pole framework covered by pressed bark or skins.

Wind brace
Any brace, such as a strut, which strengthens a structure or framework against the wind; a diagonal brace that ties rafters of a roof together to prevent racking.

Winding stair   See Stair.

Window
An opening in an exterior wall of a building to admit light and air; usually glazed; an entire assembly consisting of a window frame, its glazing, and any operating hardware.

awning window
A window consisting of a number of top-hinged horizontal sashes one above the other, the bottom edges of which swing outward; operated by one control device.

bay window
A window forming a recess in a room and projecting outwards from the wall either in a rectangular, polygonal or semicircular form. Some are supported on corbels or on projecting moldings.

bay window

blank window
A recess in an exterior wall, having the external appearance of a window; a window which has been sealed off but is still visible.

bow window
A rounded bay window projecting from the face of a wall; in plan it is a segment of a circle.

box-head window
A window constructed so that the sashes can slide vertically up into the head to provide maximum opening for ventilation.

cabinet window
A type of projecting window or bay window for the display of goods in shops.

camber window
A window arched at the top.

cant window
A bay window erected on a plan of canted outlines; the sides are not at right angles to the wall.

casement window
A window ventilating sash, fixed at the sides of the opening into which it is fitted, which swings open on hinges along its entire length.

coupled window
Two closely spaced windows which form a pair.

crippled window
A dormer window.

dormer window
A vertical window which projects from a sloping roof, placed in a small gable.

double-hung window
A window having two vertically sliding sashes, each closing a different part of the window; the weight of each sash is counterbalanced for ease of opening and closing.

double window
Two windows, side by side, which form a single architectural unit.

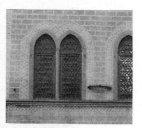

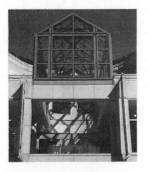

gable window
A window in a gable; a window shaped like a gable.

hopper window
A window sash which opens inward and is hinged at the bottom; when open, air passes over the top of the sash.

jalousie window
A window consisting of a series of overlapping horizontal glass louvers which pivot simultaneously in a common frame, and are actuated by one or more operating devices.

lancet window
A narrow window with a sharp pointed arch that is typical of English Gothic architecture; one light shaped in the form of a lancet window.

lattice window
A window casement, fixed or hinged, with glazing bars set diagonally.

false window
The representation of a window that is inserted in a facade to complete a series of windows or to give the appearance of symmetry.

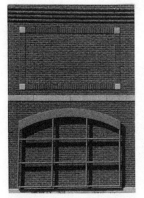

loop window
A long narrow, vertical opening, usually widening inward, cut in a medieval wall, parapet, or fortification, for use by archers.

lucarne window
A small dormer window in a roof or spire.

folding casement
One of a pair of casements, with rabbeted meeting stiles which is hung in a single frame without a mullion, and hinged together so that they can open and fold in a confined space.

operable window
A window which may be opened for ventilation, as opposed to a fixed light.

oriel window
A bay window corbeled out from a wall of an upper story; a projecting bay that forms the extension of a room, used extensively in medieval English residential architecture.

ox-eye window
A round or oval aperture, open, louvered, or glazed; an occulus or oeil-de-boeuf.

ox-eye window

picture window
A large fixed pane of glass, often between two narrower operable windows, usually located to present the most attractive view to the exterior.

pivoting window
A window having a sash which rotates about fixed vertical or horizontal pivots, located at or toward the center, in contrast to one hung on hinges along an edge.

ribbon window
One of a horizontal series of windows, separated only by mullions, which forms a horizontal band across the facade of a building.

rose window
A large, circular medieval window, containing tracery disposed in a radial manner.

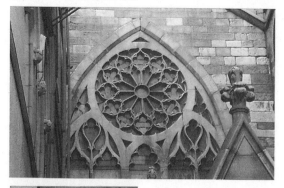

roundel
A small circular panel or window; an oculus, a bull's eye or circular light like the bottom of a bottle.

shed dormer window
A dormer window whose eave line is parallel to the eave line of the main roof instead of gabled to provide more attic space.

sliding sash window
A window which moves horizontally in grooves or between runners at the top and bottom of the window frame.

stained-glass window
A window whose glass is colored.

venetian window
A large window, characteristic of neoclassical styles, divided by columns or piers resembling pilasters into three lights, the middle one of which is usually wider that the others, and sometimes arched at the head,

vertically pivoted window
A window having a sash which pivots about a vertical axis at or near its center; when opened, the outside glass surface is conveniently accessible for cleaning.

vertical sliding window
A window having one or more sashes which move only in the vertical direction; they are held in various open positions by means of friction or a rachet device instead of being supported by a counterweight.

wheel window
A large circular window in which the tracery radiates from the center; a variety of the rose window.

Window casing
The finished frame surrounding a window; the visible frame; usually consists of wood, metal, or stone.

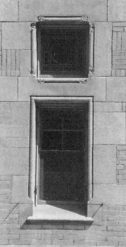

Window frame
The fixed, nonoperable frame of a window, consisting of two jambs, a head and a sill, designed to receive and hold the sash or casement and all necessary hardware.

Window head
A horizontal cross member at the top of a window frame, in a variety of forms, as semicircles, arches or triangular shapes. Some have decorative moldings on the head and jambs, while sills are left plain to shed water.

Windowlight
A pane of glass which has been installed in a window,

Window mullion
A vertical member between the lights of a window.

Window muntin
A rabbeted member for holding the edges of windowpanes within a sash.

Windowpane
One of the divisions of a window or door, consisting of a single unit of glass set in a frame.

Window seat
A seat built into the inside bottom of a window.

Window sill
The horizontal member at the base of a window opening.

Window unit
A complete window, with sashes or casements. ready for shipment or installation in a building.

Window wall
A type of curtain wall, usually composed of vertical and horizontal metal framing members containing fixed lights, operable windows or opaque panels, or a combination thereof.

Wing
A subsidiary part of a building extending out from the main portion.

Winged bull
A winged human-headed bull of colossal size, usually guarding in pairs, the portals of ancient Assyrian palaces as a symbol of force and domination.

Wire glass See Glass.

Wivern See animal forms.

Wood
The hard, fibrous substance which composes the trunk and branches of a tree, lying between the pitch and the bark.

birch
A moderately strong, high-density wood, yellowish to brown in color; its uniform texture and figure are well suited for veneer, flooring, and turned wood products.

cedar
A highly aromatic, moderately high-density, fine-textured wood of a distinctive red color with white streaks; widely used for fence posts, shingles, and mothproof closet linings.

cherry
An even-textured, moderately high-density wood, rich red-brown in color; takes a high luster, and is used for cabinetwork and paneling.

chestnut
A light, coarse-grained, medium-hard wood, used for ornamental work and trim.

cypress
A moderately strong, hard, and heavy softwood; its heartwood is naturally decay-resistant, and is used for exterior and interior construction where durability is required.

douglas fir
A strong, medium-density, medium-textured softwood; widely used for plywood and as lumber and timber in construction.

ebony
Wood of a number of tropical species, usually distinguished by its dark color, durability, and hardness; used for carving ornamental cabinetwork.

elm
A tough, strong, moderately high-density hardwood of brown color; often has a twisted interlocked grain; used for decorative veneer, piles and planks.

fir
A softwood of the temperate climates including douglas fir, white fir, silver fir, balsam fir; used for framing and interior trim.

gum
A moderately high-density hardwood, whitish to gray-green in color and of uniform texture; used for low-grade veneer, plywood, and rough cabinet work.

hemlock
Wood of a coniferous tree; moisture-resistant. soft, coarse, uneven-textured, splinters easily, inferior for construction use.

hickory
A tough, hard, strong wood; has high shock resistance and high bending strength.

larch, tamerack
A fine-textured, strong, hard, straight-grained wood of a coniferous tree; heavier than most softwoods.

limba
A straight-grained, fine textured wood used for interior paneling.

locust, black and red
Wood of the locust tree; coarse-grained. strong, hard, decay-resistant, and durable.

mahogany
A straight-grained wood of intermediate density, pinkish to red-brown in color; used primarily for interior cabinetwork and decorative paneling.

maple
A hard, tough, moderately high-density wood, light to dark brown in color; has a uniform texture; used for flooring, and wood trim.

oak
A tough, hard, high-density wood; coarse-textured, ranging in color from light tan to pink or brown; used for both structural and decorative applications, such as framing timbers, flooring, and plywood.

pine
A wood of a number of species of coniferous evergreens; may be divided into two classes; soft pine and hard pitch pine; an important source of construction lumber and plywood.

redwood
A durable, straight-grained, high-strength, low-density softwood; especially resistant to decay and insect attack; light red to deep reddish-brown in color; used primarily for construction, plywood, and millwork.

satinwood
A hard, fine-grained, pale to golden yellow wood of the acacia gum tree; used in cabinetwork and decorative paneling.

spruce
A white to light brown or red-brown, straight and even-grained wood; moderately low density and strength; relatively inexpensive; used for general utility lumber.

teak
A dark golden yellow or brown wood with a greenish or black cast, moderately hard, coarse-grained, very durable; immune to the attack of insects; used for construction, plywood and decorative paneling.

tulipwood
A soft, close-textured durable wood, yellowish in color; used for millwork and veneer.

white oak
A hard, heavy, durable wood, gray to reddish-brown in color; especially used for flooring, paneling, and trim.

white pine
A soft, light wood which works easily; does not split when nailed; does not swell or warp appreciably; is widely used in building construction.

yellow pine
A hard resinous wood of the longleaf pine tree, having dark bands of summerwood alternating with lighter-colored springwood; used as flooring and in general construction.

Wood-frame construction
Construction in which exterior walls, bearing walls and partitions, floor and roof constructions, and their supports are of wood or other combustible material; when it does not qualify as heavy-timber construction.

clapboard siding
A wood siding commonly used as an exterior covering on a building of frame construction, applied horizontally and overlapped, with the grain running lengthwise, thicker along the lower edge than the upper.

folded plate
A thin skin of plywood reinforced by purlins to form structures of great strength.

glue-laminated arch
An arch made from layers of wood that are joined with adhesives. The glued joints transmit the shear stresses, so the structure acts as one piece capable of use as structural arches and long-span beams.

Masonite
Trade name of a brand of tempered pressed board.

particleboard
A large class of building boards made from wood particles compressed in a binder; often faced with a veneer.

plywood
An engineered panel composed of an odd number of thin sheets permanently bonded together, sometimes faced with a veneer.

shake
Any thick hand-split edge-grained shingle or clapboard, formed by splitting a short log into tapered sections.

shingle
A roofing unit of wood, asphalt material, slate, tile, concrete, asbestos cement, or other material that is cut to stock dimensions and thicknesses and used as an overlapping covering over sloping roofs and side walls.

shiplap siding
Wood sheathing whose edges are rabbeted to make an overlapping joint.

stressed skin panel
A panel constructed of plywood and seasoned lumber; the simple framing and plywood skin act as a total unit to resist loads.

veneer
A thin sheet of wood that has been sliced, rotary-cut, or sawn from a log; used as one of several plies in plywood for added strength or as facing material on less attractive wood.

Woodwork
Work produced by the carpenter's and joiner's art, applied to parts or objects in wood rather than to the complete structure.

Working Drawings
Drawings, intended for use by a contractor, subcontractor, or fabricator, which forms part of the contract documents for a building; contains the necessary information to manufacture or erect an object or structure.

Wrightian style
The architecture (1900–1959) of Frank Lloyd Wright, for which this style is named, was characterized first by the prairie-style house. The long, low buildings with broad overhanging low-pitched roofs and rows of casement windows emphasized the house's horizontal relationship with the site. It culminated in the building of Taliesin, his home and school. A second period began with innovative house designs such as Fallingwater. A third period provided architectural forms based on geometric shapes, such as the hexagon, octagon, circles and arcs. The spiral form of the Guggenheim Museum is the best known of this period. Later work includes a series of decorative concrete block houses and a new desert house, Taliesin West. His career covered over 400 buildings and an equal number of unrealized projects.

Wrightian Style

Wrought-iron work
Iron that is hammered or
forged into shape, either
when hot or cold, usually
decorative.

Y·y

Yurt

A circular tentlike dwelling, usually movable, used by nations of northern and central Asia, constructed of skins stretched over a wooden framework.

Z·z

Zapotec architecture

This eclectic architecture (700–900) is found in Oaxaca, Mexico. The Zapotecs assimilated influences from the Olmecs (700–300 B.C.) and especially from Teotihuacan (300–900 A.D.). It culminated in a recognizable regional style, characterized by pyramids having several stepped terraces, accented with balustrades whose tops were decorated. One of the most notable sites is Monte Alban, a carefully planned ceremonial complex.

Ziggurat

A Mesopotamian temple having the form of a terraced pyramid rising in three to seven successively receding stages in height, built of mud brick, featuring an outside staircase and a shrine at the top.

Zigzag

A line formed by angles that alternately project and retreat; occurring in bands, on columns, and in larger patterns on cornices.

Zoophoric column
A column bearing a figure or figures of one or more men or animals.

Zoophorus
A horizontal band bearing carved figures, animals or persons, especially a sculptured Ionic frieze.

Zoophorus

Zwinger
The protective fortress of a city; the modern name of several German palaces, or parts of palaces.

244

INDEX

Fretting 94
Fretwork 94
Frieze 94
Frontispiece 94
Frosted 94
Functionalism 95
Funk architecture 95
Futurist style 95

G • g

Gable 95
Gabled tower 96
Gable roof 185
Gable window 236
Gaine 96
Gallery 96
Gambrel roof 185
Garage 96
Garden 96
Garden apartment 96
Garden house 96
Gargoyle 96
Garland 97
Garret 97
Gate 97
Gate house 98
Gate tower 98
Gateway 98
Gauged brick 36
Gazebo 98
Geminated 98
Geminated capital 43
Geodesic dome 72
Geometric style 98
Geometric tracery 220
Geometrical 99
Georgian architecture 99
Gesso 99
Gibbs Surround 99
Gilding 99
Gingerbread 99
Gingerbread style 99
Girder 100
Girdle 100
Girt 100
Glass 100
Glass block 101
Glass door 75
Glass mullion system 102

Glaze 102
Glazed brick 36
Glazed tile 218
Glazed work 102
Glue-laminated arch 241
Glyph 177
Gneiss 207
Gold leaf 102
Gold size 102
Gopuram gate 97
Gorgoneion 102
Gothic arch 16
Gothic architecture 102
Gothic Revival style 103
Gouache 103
Granite 207
Greek architecture 103
Greek Revival style 104
Greenhouse 104
Grid 104
Grid-based organization 146
Griffin 9
Grille 104
Grillwork 105
Groin 105
Groin arch 16
Groined rib 105
Grotesque 105
Grotto 105
Ground joint 138
Ground line 157
Ground plane 157
Ground sill 106
Grouped columns 55
Grouped pilasters 160
Grout 106
Grouted masonry 106
Guest house 106
Guilloche molding 137
Gum 240
Gupta 106
Gusset 106
Gutta 106
Gutter 106
Gymnasium 106
Gypsum board 106

H • h

Hacienda 106

Half column 55
Half-round molding 137
Half-space landing 121
Half-timbered 106
Half-timbered wall 232
Hallway 106
Hammer beam 30
Hammer brace 106
Handrail 107
Hanger 107
Harmonic proportion 107
Harmony 107
Haunch 107
Haunch arch 17
Head 107
Header 107
Head mortar joint 138
Hearthstone 107
Heavy-timber construction 107
Helix 107
Hellenic architecture 107
Hellenistic architecture 107
Hemispherical 107
Hemlock 240
Henry II style 108
Henry IV style 108
Herm 108
Herringbone 108
Hexagonal 108
Hickory 240
Hierarchy 108
Hieroglyph 108
High relief 177
High Renaissance 109
High rise 109
Hinge 109
Hip 109
Hip knob 147
Hip rafter 173
Hip roof 185
Hipped end 109
Hipped gable 109
Hipped gable 95
Hittite architecture 109
Hollow core door 75
Hollow molding 137
Hollow square molding 137
Hollyhock ornament 147
Homestead 109